Fig 6

Fig 7

Fig 8   Fig 9

Fig 13

Fig. 14

Fig 12

Fig. 22

Fig 19

Fig 24.

Fig 23

Fig 27.

Fig. 25.

B. FRANKLIN, PRINTER

Benjamin Franklin at about sixty, from an engraving, c. 1900, based on an earlier portrait

B. FRANKLIN, PRINTER

DAVID A. ADLER

HOLIDAY HOUSE / New York

For Dad

Maps by Heather Saunders

The text typeface is Caslon Antique. Caslon was a typeface frequently
used by Benjamin Franklin at his press in Philadelphia.
The ornament on the title page and all the rules under the running heads
were reproduced from *The History of Joseph*,
printed and sold by B. Franklin in 1739.
The chapter opening ornament is also
from Franklin's press.
It is from *An Alarm Sounded*
by Job Noble, printed in 1740.
The endpapers are Franklin's maritime ideas,
sent in a letter to Alphonsus Le Roy,
a friend in Paris.

www.holidayhouse.com

First Edition

Library of Congress Cataloging-in-Publication Data
Adler, David A.
B. Franklin, printer / David A. Adler.—1st ed.
p. cm.
Includes bibliographical references and index.
ISBN 0-8234-1675-5
1. Franklin, Benjamin, 1706–1790—Juvenile literature.
2. Statesmen—United States—Biography—Juvenile literature.
3. Printers—United States—Biography—Juvenile literature.
4. Inventors—United States—Biography—Juvenile literature.
5. Scientists—United States—Biography—Juvenile literature.
[1. Franklin, Benjamin, 1706–1790. 2. Statesmen.
3. Printers. 4. Scientists.] I. Title.
E302.6.F8 A26 2001
973.3'092—dc21
[B]   2001024535

ABOUT THE TITLE

In 1728, at the age of twenty-two,
Benjamin Franklin
wrote his own epitaph:

The Body of
B Franklin, Printer,
(Like the Cover of an old Book
Its Contents torn out
And stript of its Lettering & Gilding)
Lies here, Food for Worms.
But the Work shall not be lost;
For it will, (as he believ'd) appear once more,
In a new and more elegant Edition
Revised and corrected;
By the Author.

Even with all his later accomplishments,
he never changed his epitaph.
He wished to be remembered as
B. Franklin, printer.

ABOUT THE QUOTES FROM FRANKLIN'S WRITINGS

I quote Franklin and his contemporaries often in this biography, in the hope my readers will get to know more than what Benjamin Franklin accomplished, they will get to know Benjamin Franklin himself. He followed the eighteenth-century tradition of spelling, so many words in these excerpts are spelled differently from the way we spell them today. He was also a great fan of phonetic spelling. In 1786 he wrote to his sister Jane Mecom, "The bad Spelling, or what is call'd so, is generally the best, as conforming to the Sound of the Letters and of the Words." He gave, as an example, a man who found these words in a letter: *Not finding Brown at home, I delivard your messeg to his yf.* According to Franklin, the man could not decipher the last word, *yf,* until his chambermaid told him it spelled *wife.* "And, indeed," Franklin wrote, "it is a much better, as well as shorter method of spelling *Wife;* than by *doubleyou, i, ef, e,* which in reality spells *doubleyifey."*

There are also differences in grammar, punctuation, and capitalization.

CONTENTS

FRANKLIN'S TRAVELS

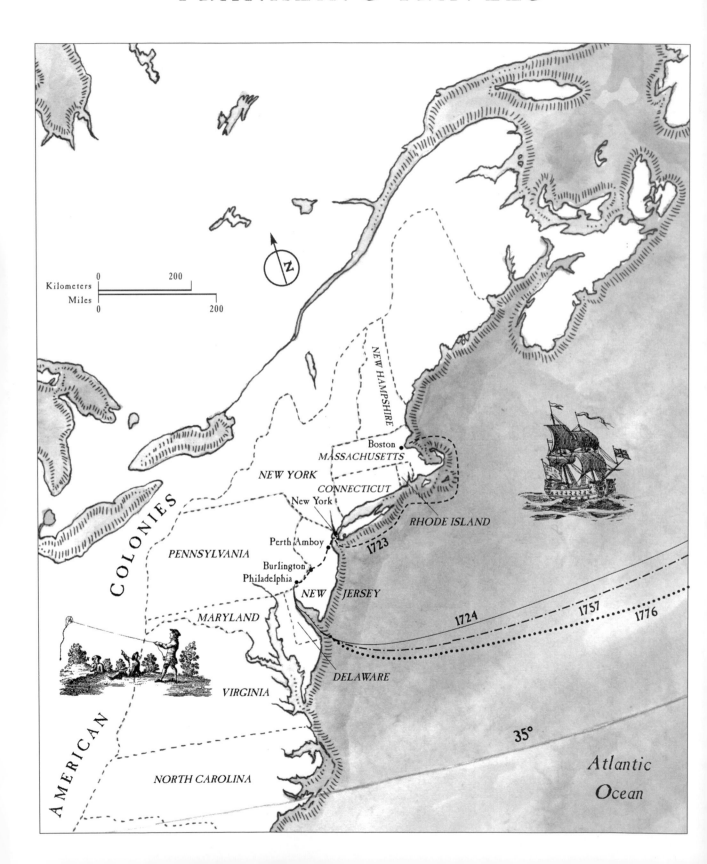

Kilometers
0   200

Miles
0   200

N

NEW HAMPSHIRE

Boston
MASSACHUSETTS

NEW YORK

CONNECTICUT

New York

RHODE ISLAND

COLONIES

Perth Amboy

1723

PENNSYLVANIA

Burlington

Philadelphia

NEW JERSEY

MARYLAND

1724   1757   1776

DELAWARE

VIRGINIA

AMERICAN

35°

NORTH CAROLINA

Atlantic
Ocean

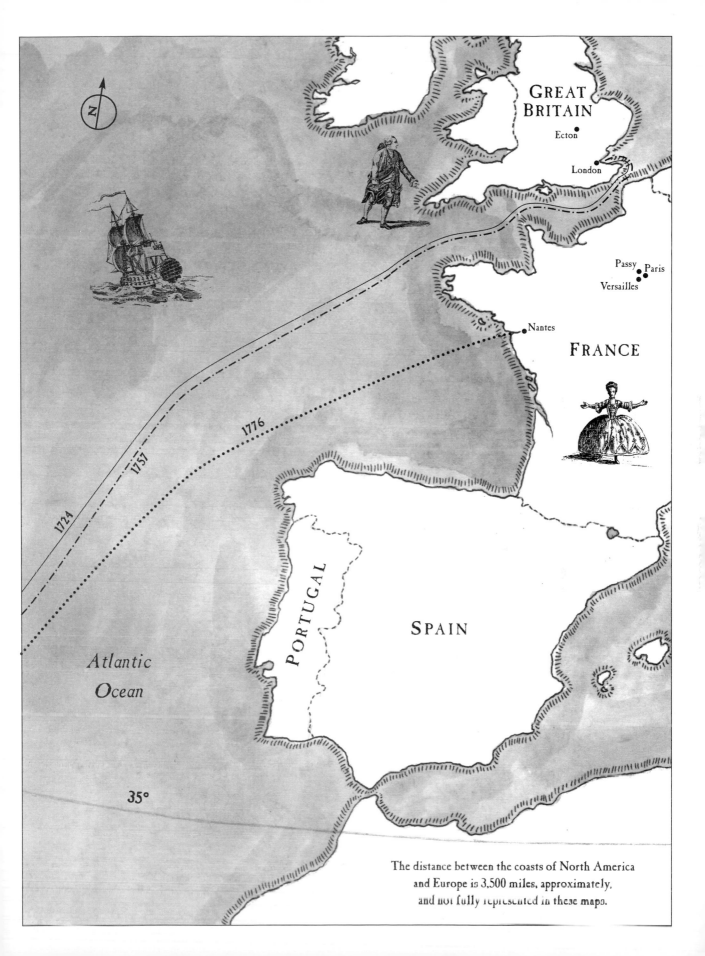

N

GREAT
BRITAIN

Ecton

London

Passy · Paris

Versailles

Nantes

FRANCE

1776

1757

1724

PORTUGAL

SPAIN

*Atlantic
Ocean*

35°

The distance between the coasts of North America
and Europe is 3,500 miles, approximately,
and not fully represented in these maps.

1.

MORE A KING

Benjamin Franklin was a singular man with a keen mind that "soared above the clouds." Still, he was modest and proud of his working-class roots. Even as a seventy-year-old diplomat in fashionable Paris, he refused to act the "dandy" and dress in fancy clothes.

"Figure to yourself an old man," Franklin wrote in a 1777 letter, "with grey hair appearing under a Martin fur cap among the powder'd heads of Paris." But in March 1778, Franklin was about to meet King Louis XVI. There were definite rules of dress when standing before the king of France, among them that a man must have his head covered with a proper powdered wig.

Benjamin Franklin ordered a wig from one of the finest Paris wig makers. His head was measured, and when the wig was ready it was brought to him. The Frenchman pulled and tugged at the wig but could not get it to fit. Franklin suggested that perhaps it was

Franklin in Paris, from an engraving by H. B. Hall, c. 1860, based on a portrait by John Trumbull (1756–1843)

1

too small. "Monsieur, it is impossible," the Frenchman said. He tried some more and then declared, "No, Monsieur. It is not the wig which is too small. It is your head which is too big."

Franklin had enough of wig makers and wigs and decided to go bare-headed. He traveled by horse-drawn carriage to the courtyard of Versailles, the king's magnificent 1,300-room palace. A crowd surrounded his carriage. When Benjamin Franklin stepped out, the people gasped. Then they cheered his daring. They saw his uncovered head as a statement of principle, a call for freedom. They called him an "Apostle of Liberty."

Even King Louis XVI approved. He told Benjamin Franklin, "I am exceedingly satisfied, in particular, with your conduct during your residence in my kingdom."

Later, when his wig troubles became known, the people of Paris said of Franklin, "He has a big head, and a great head."

Benjamin Franklin truly did have a great head. And he was a man of great accomplishments.

He was a printer, scientist, inventor, and statesman. He was Amer-

King Louis XVI of France,
from an engraving by Pelée, c. 1880,
based on an earlier portrait

A French engraving, "America Set Free by Franklin," c. 1780

ica's first great popular writer. He organized Philadelphia's police force and fire company and our country's first subscription library. And he was the only man to have signed the Declaration of Independence, the Constitution, the treaty with France that helped win the Revolution, and the treaty with England that ended it.

During his stay in Paris, Benjamin Franklin was affectionately called "Le Grand Franklin"—The Great Franklin. Many years later, at the unveiling of a statue honoring him, the newspaperman Horace Greeley spoke of Franklin's time in France. In the "gilded salons of Versailles, where modest Benjamin Franklin stood," Greeley said, he was "in fact more a king than the gentle Louis."

2.

THE FRANKLINS

Benjamin Franklin was born in Boston in a four-room house on Milk Street. He was born on Sunday, January 17, 1706. Later that day, his father, Josiah Franklin, carried him through the snow from a fierce storm that had hit the city just three days before, across the street, to the Old South Church, where Benjamin was baptized.

Boston then was the trading, business, and cultural center of the colonies. Sailing ships loaded with slaves, cloth, molasses, rum, tobacco, and farm tools docked in Boston harbor. Farmers brought their crops of

Josiah Franklin taking his newborn son to be baptized, from a drawing by Victor A. Searles, c. 1897

The Franklin house on Milk Street, c. 1890, based on an earlier drawing

grains and fruits there to be sold and sent off in sailing ships across the Atlantic to foreign ports or to colonies farther south. Lumbermen shipped timber to the West Indies and trappers sold skins from raccoons, beavers, and other animals to be used to make coats, hats, and blankets.

Boston was a city of some six thousand people, who lived in houses built mostly of wood. In their yards they grew vegetables and kept cows, chickens, and pigs. In daylight, the streets were busy with horsemen, people pushing wheelbarrows, carts, and wagons, children playing, and stray animals. At night, there was danger in the streets of being run down by a galloping horseman or of being robbed.

The Franklins were new to Boston. Benjamin's father was born in England on the same thirty acres in Ecton, a village in Northamptonshire,

A southeast view of colonial Boston, from an engraving by William Price, c. 1739

where his family had lived for more than three hundred years. Their place was just a few miles from the ancestral home of George Washington. But while the Washingtons were knights, abbots, and lord-of-the-manor types, the Franklins of Ecton were blacksmiths and tradesmen.

The English Franklins were religious people, many of them stubborn and independent. They were among the earliest Protestants and held to their beliefs even when that was dangerous, through the cruel reign of Mary I (1553–1558), the Roman Catholic queen of England. She was called "Bloody Mary," and during her reign some three hundred religious independents were burned at the stake.

Benjamin's great-great-grandfather lived during Queen Mary's reign and kept a Protestant Bible under the lid of a stool. Whenever he read from it, he kept one of his children at the door to look out for informers. When one was spotted, the elder Franklin would put the Bible back and close the lid.

Benjamin's grandfather, Thomas Franklin, surrounded his nine children with the words of the Bible by painting them on the inside walls of his house.

Benjamin's father was also religious and rebellious. He didn't attend the established church. Josiah Franklin went to religious services in private homes and used an unauthorized prayer book when both of these actions were strictly against the law.

In 1683, when he was twenty-five, Josiah Franklin left Ecton to seek religious freedom in America. He crossed the Atlantic with his wife, Anne, and their three children. They settled in Boston.

When he came to Boston, Josiah Franklin first worked as a dyer. But people there weren't too particular about the color of their cloth, so he became a soap and candle maker and did a brisk business. Even in rustic Boston, people needed soap, and during the long, dark winter nights, they needed plenty of candles.

Josiah Franklin had other interests, too. He played the violin, sang, drew pictures, and was handy with a hammer. He was well informed. Benjamin later wrote of his father, "I remember well his being frequently visited by leading people, who consulted him for his opinion in affairs of the town or the church he belonged to, and showed a good deal of respect for his judgement and advice."

Josiah and Anne had seven children—Elizabeth, Samuel, Hannah, Josiah, Anne, Joseph, and another Joseph. Both sons named Joseph died soon after they were born. Josiah's wife died, too, in 1689, while giving birth to the second Joseph.

Within several months, thirty-one-year-old Josiah married twenty-two-year-old Abiah Folger, the daughter of Peter Folger, an independent, principled man who spoke out for religious freedom and taught Native Americans how to read and write.

"She was a discreet and virtuous woman," Benjamin wrote of his mother. She was strong and hearty. She took care of Josiah's five children and bore him ten more—John, Peter, Mary, James, Sarah, Ebenezer, Thomas, Benjamin, Lydia, and Jane. Benjamin later remembered seeing as many as twelve of his brothers and sisters sitting around the table at dinnertime. "We were fed plentifully, made comfortable with fire and clothing," Benjamin's sister Jane later wrote. "All was harmony."

Among the Franklin children, young Benjamin stood out as especially smart. Soon after he learned how to talk, he taught himself how to read. It became his favorite pastime. In the early eighteenth century, there were no public libraries in the American colonies. Books were expensive and scarce. Of the few available, many were about religion, so at five, Benjamin read the Bible. After that, he read mostly volumes of ministers' sermons.

Josiah was pleased to see his son reading sermons. It was considered proper to give a tithe, one-tenth of your earnings, to the church. In that spirit, Josiah planned that Benjamin, his tenth son, would serve the church. He would study theology at Harvard and become a minister.

As a first step toward the ministry, Benjamin was sent at eight to the Boston Latin School. But Josiah Franklin soon realized his son was not meant to be a preacher. The boy had no patience for prayers, even the few words of thanks said before each meal. Benjamin once suggested to his father that he simply say grace once, over an entire cask of salted meat, and be done with it.

Josiah took Benjamin out of Boston Latin School and sent him to George Brownwell's school. Benjamin did well there in writing, but he remembered later, "I failed in arithmetic and made no progress in it."

When Benjamin was ten, his father removed him from school altogether and put him to work in his soap and candle shop. There Benjamin cut wicks for the candles, filled the dripping molds, helped look after the shop, and ran errands. But, even out of school, Benjamin continued to learn. Now he took his lessons from life.

Benjamin and his young friends often fished for minnows by a marsh on the outskirts of Boston. One day, when the area became muddy, they took stones from a nearby building site and piled them by the water's edge so they could keep their feet dry. The next morning the workmen found that stones were missing. "We were discovered," Benjamin wrote. "Several of us were corrected by our fathers, and, though I pleaded the usefulness of the work, mine convinced me that nothing was useful which was not honest."

Benjamin learned, too, from his own experiments. "When I was a boy," he later wrote, "I made two oval pallets, each about ten inches long and six broad, with a hole for the thumb. . . . I swam faster by means of these pallets, but they fatigued my wrists."

Another swimming experiment was more successful. He tied one end of a string to a paper kite and the other to a stick. "Lying on my back and holding the stick in my hands, I was drawn along the surface of the water in a very agreeable manner. . . . I began to cross the pond with my kite, which carried me quite over without the least fatigue, and with

While a friend watches, Franklin experiments using a kite to pull him across the water, from a drawing by Victor A. Searles, c. 1897

the greatest pleasure imaginable."

In his father's soap and candle shop, Benjamin learned to work hard. But he later wrote, "I dislik'd the Trade, and had a Strong Inclination for the sea."

This frightened Josiah Franklin. His son Josiah was already a sailor. After nine years without a word, Josiah returned with tales of adventure in far-off India. Benjamin wrote that his father feared if he did not find an "agreeable" trade for him, "I should break away and get to sea."

Josiah showed Benjamin bricklayers, blacksmiths, cabinetmakers, roofers, brass workers, and coopers at work. Then when Benjamin didn't choose a trade, Josiah chose one for him. He would become a cutler, a maker of scissors and knives. He sent the boy to his nephew Samuel Franklin, the one surviving child of Josiah's brother Benjamin. But when Samuel asked to be paid to train his cousin, Josiah took him home again.

Next, Josiah decided that since twelve-year-old Benjamin loved to read, he should become a printer. Benjamin's older brother James had just returned from England with type and a printing press and was setting up shop on Queen's Street, next door to the jail. Benjamin was made his apprentice. He signed a contract to work for nine years, until he was twenty-one, in exchange for a room, food to eat, some clothing, training as a printer, and a little pay during his last year of service.

Benjamin Franklin was proud of the trade his father chose for him, so proud that in 1728, when he wrote his own epitaph, he decided he wanted to be remembered for eternity as "B Franklin, Printer."

3.

APPRENTICE PRINTER

During his apprenticeship, Benjamin would wake early and dress in a coarse shirt, leather pants, and high blue wool socks. He would work ten, twelve, or sometimes fourteen hours a day. He swept his brother's shop, kept the fire in the fireplace going, ran errands, sorted and set type, and inked and ran the press.

James Franklin, who was not married, paid a nearby family to feed him, his brother, and his other apprentices. Benjamin wrote later that when he was sixteen, he learned to prepare some dishes, "boiling potatoes or rice, making hasty pudding, and a few others and then proposed to my brother that if he would give me, weekly, half the money he paid for my board, I would board myself."

James quickly agreed.

When the others went off to eat, Benjamin remained in the printing house. At the time, he was a vegetarian and his meals were often "no more than a biscuit or a slice of bread, a handful of raisins, or a tart from the pastry-cook's, and a glass of water." With this light diet, Benjamin spent

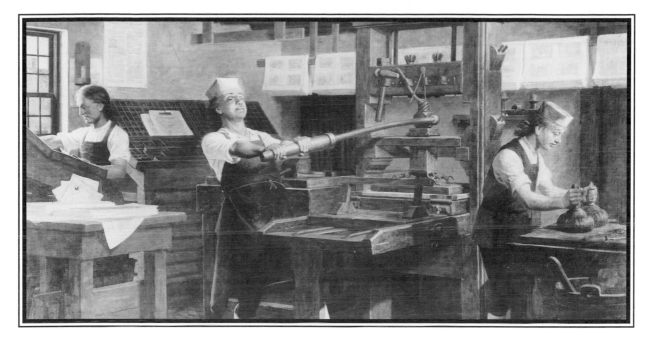

Benjamin Franklin working as an apprentice in his brother's print shop, from a painting by Charles E. Mills, c. 1910

only half the money his brother gave him for food. He used what money was left to buy books.

"From a child," Benjamin later wrote, "I was fond of reading, and all the little money that came into my hands was ever laid out in books."

There were perhaps as many as ten bookshops in Boston, quite a lot for a place where most of what was sold came from across the ocean. Benjamin bought some books and borrowed others from the booksellers' apprentices. Many times, he sat up through much of the night to finish a borrowed book so that he could return it in the morning, before the bookseller noticed it was missing. He read books on navigation, arithmetic, English grammar, philosophy, religion, and health.

"Another bookish lad," according to Franklin, was his good friend John Collins. The two boys argued often, once over whether women could be taught certain sciences. Benjamin thought they could. John Collins disagreed. They parted without settling the issue, and since they would not see each other for a while, they continued their discussion in a series of letters.

The debate ended when Benjamin's father found the letters.

Benjamin Franklin selling ballads, from a drawing by Victor A. Searles, c. 1897

Josiah Franklin ignored the arguments. "He took occasion to talk to me about the manner of my writing," Benjamin later wrote. He said, though Benjamin had the advantage in spelling and punctuation, he "fell far short in elegance of expression.... I saw the justice of his remarks and thence grew more attentive to the manner in writing and determined to endeavor at improvement."

He did improve and soon James Franklin put his brother to work writing. He set Benjamin to composing ballads that James printed and sold. One about a shipwreck in Boston harbor and another about the capture and hanging of a famous pirate were big sellers.

Later, James printed more of Benjamin's creative work. But James had no idea it was his brother's writing.

James became the printer of the *Boston Gazette*, the second newspaper after the *Boston News-Letter* regularly published in the colonies. Printing the *Gazette* was an important addition to his business, so James was upset when, after just forty issues, he lost the job to another printer. To keep his presses busy, James started a newspaper of his own, the *New-England Courant*.

James Franklin's *Courant* was a spirited newspaper. James and friends of his who wrote for it became embroiled in a debate with a Puritan firebrand minister, the Reverend Increase Mather, over inoculations against smallpox, a dreaded disease of the time. They called the inoculations dangerous "hocus-pocus" medicine and published their arguments, sometimes sharply worded, in the *Courant*.

The Reverend Mather was for inoculations and defended his son

Cotton's use of them during an outbreak of smallpox. He called the *Courant* a "wicked paper," a sign of the coming downfall of Boston. He warned that, if the newspaper was not stopped, "I am afraid that some awful judgement will come upon this land, and the wrath of God will arise and there will be no remedy." He wondered what reason James Franklin would give "the Judgement seat of God...for printing things so vile and abominable."

James's friends also wrote letters and essays for the newspaper that made fun of the fancy people of Boston and celebrated the charms of its young women. They signed their pieces with made-up names such as Tom Tram, Ichabod Henroost, Tabitha Talkative, Abigail Afterwit, and Homespun Jack.

The "war of words" with the Reverend Mather and the brash letters and essays from James Franklin's friends stirred real interest in the *Courant*. With all the excitement, Benjamin was eager to write for his brother's paper. He soon did.

One morning a letter was found by the door of the print shop. It was signed *Mrs. Silence Dogood*, but was written in secret by sixteen-year-old Benjamin Franklin. Over the next six months, he wrote fourteen Dogood letters. In them he proposed that women be educated and that there be some insurance to help poor widows. He made fun of women's fashions. He had great fun, too, with the young men attending Harvard: "A great many," he wrote, "were little better than blockheads and dunces," and its graduates "lived as poor as church mice, being unable to dig, and ashamed to beg, and to live by their wits was impossible."

When the first letter was discovered, Benjamin listened as James and his friends discussed who might

Benjamin Franklin slipping a Silence Dogood letter under the door of his brother's print shop, from a drawing by Victor A. Searles, c. 1897

On the 15th Instant, *James Jarvies,* Blacksmith, (who used to be taken with Fits of the Falling Sickness) being Shoveling of Snow at his Well in the Yard, on a sudden his head foremost fell into the Well, his own journey-man Shovelling Snow in the same Yard heard a sudden noise, & immediately cried out, & several persons got to the Well where nothing was to be seen but his feet, and got him out, who spoke but very few words afterwards, and dyed within a few hours.

—January 15, 1705

On Wednesday morning the 17th Instant, dyed *Elizabeth Whetlie,* Single Woman, for want of help, being big with Child, who would not own that she was with Child, was afterwards opened, and found to be so.

—January 15, 1705

We have now alive and in good health at the Merchant Taylors Alms-House on Little Tower Hill, Anne Scrimpshaw the Daughter of Thomas Scrimpshaw Wool Stapler; She was born in the Parish of St. Mary Le Bow London, April the 3d Anno Domini 1584, being now 127 Years of Age, and so great a Rarity that Her Majesty was pleased to make her a Visit.

—January 14, 1711

This Town that has been sorely afflicted with the Measils and Feaver for some Months past, is now thro Mercy pretty well restored to its former Health.

—January 18, 1713

On Thursday night last a Fire broke out in Back Street and burnt down Mr. *Blunt* Tallow Chandler, his Work-House. That night and next Day and Night we had an Easterly Storm of Wind and Snow.

On Friday night one *Bacon* of Roxbury, going home in his Slade with three Horses, was Bewilder'd in the Dark, himself found Dead with the Cold next Morning, one of the Horses drowned in the Marsh, the other two not yet heard of.

—January 25, 1713

At a Court of Assize held here the first Tuesday of May last, a certain Person convict of Forging, Counterfeiting and Uttering Five Twenty Shilling Bills of Credit, of the Province, and putting off the said Forged and Counterfeit Bills or some of them, at the value of True Bills of Credit, was Ordered and Sentenced by the said Court to be set upon the Pillory in the Market Place near the Town House on Thursday the 27th of May, have one of his Ears cut off, Branded on the Right Cheek with the letter F, and

suffer Twelve Months Imprisonment &c. Which was accordingly put in Execution on the said Day.

—May 31, 1714

On the 15th Currant, in Letters and Prints brought by Two Vessels arriving here, one from Great Britain, and the other from Cork in Ireland, we received the Sorrowful News of the death of Our Late Most Gracious Soverign Lady Queen ANNE of Blessed Memory, And of the Accession of the Most High and Mighty Prince GEORGE, Elector of Brunswick Luneburg, to the Crown of Great-Britain &c. —September 13, 1714

On Friday & Saturday last we had here very great Rain; and it is very remarkable that all this Summer we have not had one Week without some Rain.

—July 25, 1715

By Letters from South Carolina of June the 30th We are informed, That they are still daily Battling with the Indian Enemy, wherein they have lost a great many Whites & Blacks, and unless some speedy help comes not to their relief, they're afraid it will soon become Indian Country. —August 8, 1715

We are inform'd from North Carolina, That Col. *Moore* who went thence to South Carolina with Forces to their

Assistance against the Indian Enemy, coming to an English Plantation, where he expected to meet English, he found about 70 of the Indians, whom he mistrusted to have killed the Planter and his Family, upon which he Tortur'd Two of the Indians in order to make 'em confess, but they would not, the Third fearing the same punishment, confessed that they Murdered the Planter and his Family, upon which Col. *Moore* kill'd and took Prisoners all the rest, the Prisoners he sent in Vessels by Water to Charlstoun.   —August 29, 1715

On Thursday last His Excellency our Governour was pleased to Issue forth a Proclamation, for Public Thanksgiving to be Observed throughout this Province upon Thursday the Seventeenth of November next.
                    —October 24, 1715

By several letters and Prints from England we are informed, That there was a Terrible, Hellish Plot and Conspiracy laid, to have cut off the whole Royal Family: The Tower, Exchequer, and Bank of England were all to be Siez'd. The City of London to be set on Fire in Five several Places, Insurrections to have been in several Places in England for the Pretender where he was to Land, and all on the 25th of September last; but that it pleased GOD, who has often wonderfully appeared for His People, timeously to discover the Snare, and prevent such Cruel and Monstrous Inhumane Barbarites. It is said, That One Hundred and Thirty Noblemen and Gentlemen of England, had Signed and given under their Hands, to pay each Two Thousand Pounds Sterling to the Pretender, in order to enable him to carry on the said Conspiracy of Massacre.

Advertisements

Any Person that wants to put out a Child a Nursing on the Breast, may repair to John Campbell Post-Master of Boston, and know further.
                    —February 11, 1706

A lusty white Girl aged about eleven years, her time of service for seven years to be disposed of by Mrs. *Elizabeth Hatch*, and to be seen at her House in Corn-Hill, Boston.

A Negro Man aged about 25 years to be Sold, by Mr. *Joseph Turril*, and to be seen at his House in Clark's-Square by the North Meeting House, Boston.

A Spanish Indian Girl aged about 15 years that has been five years in the Country, who speaks good English, and can do any sort of Houshold work, to be Sold, Inquire at the Post Office in Boston and know further.
                    —October 5, 1713

Dryden's Virgil in Folio with Cuts, but has forgot to whom, and the Person that Borrwow'd it is hereby desired to send it to the Post-Office in Boston, that the true owner may have it again; who will be very thankful to the Borrower.
                    —March 16, 1716

The Boston News-Letter, *the first regularly published American newspaper, began publication in 1704, with up to 300 copies printed and distributed each week. It contained news from Europe (most of it many months old), the colonies, West Indies, and Boston. It began as a single sheet of paper, 8 inches by almost 13 inches, printed on both sides. John Campbell, the postmaster of Boston, was the newspaper's publisher and the notation "Published by Authority" printed beneath the masthead meant his publication had the approval of the royal governor. Nothing critical of his rule appeared in the* News-Letter.

have written it. Their guesses centered on the more learned and talented men of Boston, and Benjamin had to hide his tears of joy and pride.

After six months, when Benjamin stopped writing the letters, someone wrote to Mrs. Dogood at the *Courant*, "Are you asleep or on a journey and cannot write?" That's when Benjamin told his brother James that he was Silence Dogood.

Benjamin was surely hoping for some show of pride from his brother. There was none. James was upset, perhaps at being upstaged. He said Benjamin was just an apprentice. All the attention his friends now paid to him would make him vain.

The next year, 1723, the *Courant* got James in trouble. He was arrested and jailed for something, "some political point," Benjamin wrote many years later, "which I have now forgotten." After a month, James was released "with an order that *James Franklin should no longer print the Paper called the New-England Courant.* There was a Consultation held in our Printing House among his Friends what he should do in this Case. Some propos'd to evade the Order by changing the Name of the Paper, but my Brother seeing the Inconveniences in that, it was finally concluded as a better Way, to let it be printed for the future under the Name of *Benjamin Franklin.*" So, seventeen-year-old Benjamin Franklin became a newspaper publisher.

If Benjamin was to be the publisher of the *Courant* instead of James, he could not be his brother's apprentice as well. Publicly, James returned the contract to his brother. But secretly, he made Benjamin sign a new one.

Benjamin didn't think James could keep him to the new secret contract. He hated working for James. They didn't get along. Benjamin resented "the blows his passion too often urged him to bestow upon me." But he also admitted, "Perhaps I was too saucy and provoking."

"Never put off till tomorrow what you can do today," Benjamin later wrote in *Poor Richard's Almanack*. He also wrote, "You may delay,

The front page of an issue of James Franklin's New-England Courant

but time will not" and "God helps them that help themselves."

After one of their fights, Benjamin helped himself. He quit his brother's shop. But he couldn't go to any of the other Boston printers for a job. His brother had told them all not to hire him. So he decided to run off.

John Collins waving good-bye as Franklin leaves for New York, from a drawing by Victor A. Searles, c. 1897

Late on the night of September 25, 1723, Benjamin boarded a ship bound for New York. At age seventeen he was making a real break with his family. His father would live another twenty-two years, but Benjamin would see him just three more times. He hardly saw his mother, either. When she died in 1752, Benjamin wrote to his sister Jane, "She has lived a good life." He also wrote, surely with some regret, "Our distance made it impracticable for us to attend her."

Benjamin later wrote in one of his almanacs, "A brother may not always be a friend but a friend will always be a brother." Perhaps he was thinking of his friend John Collins, who helped him get away.

Collins secretly booked passage for Benjamin with a made-up story. He told the captain of the ship that his friend had fallen in with a "girl of bad character." The girl's parents were determined to make him marry her, so he was running off.

Five days after Benjamin fled, this advertisement appeared in the *New-England Courant:* "James Franklin, printer in Queen's Street, wants a likely lad for an apprentice"—someone to replace Benjamin Franklin.

4.

RUNAWAY

New York, in 1723, was a town of some seven to eight thousand mostly Dutch-speaking people. The sidewalks were cobblestoned. Its streets were narrow and winding. It had no bookstore, no newspaper, and just one printer, William Bradford.

Soon after Benjamin Franklin arrived in New York, he went to see Bradford, but the printer had no need for another worker. He suggested Benjamin go to Philadelphia, where his son had a print shop, so Benjamin was on the move again.

He took passage on an old boat with rotten sails bound for Perth Amboy. His plan was to walk from Perth Amboy across New Jersey to Burlington, at the edge of the Delaware River. There he would take a boat to Philadelphia.

The water was rough. The old boat pitched wildly. It threw the only other passenger, a

The waterfront of New York City in the late seventeenth century, from a drawing by Hugo Allard, c. 1673

drunken Dutchman, overboard. Quick-thinking Benjamin reached into the water, grabbed the Dutchman by his hair, and pulled him back on board. Then the wind became so strong it threatened to destroy the boat. The boatman pulled down the sails. He dropped anchor close to the shore of Long Island and waited for a calmer wind. The boatman, Benjamin Franklin, and the Dutchman spent a sleepless night. Water sprayed over the sides of the boat and leaked through its bottom until the three men were soaked.

The next morning they set sail again, and late the next afternoon they reached Perth Amboy. From there, Benjamin walked three days to Burlington, where he boarded another boat. Then, eleven days after leaving Boston, he arrived in Philadelphia.

The kind master of the second boat didn't want his poor-looking young passenger to pay for the voyage, but Benjamin insisted. He had just one silver dollar and a few copper coins. He gave the boatman the copper coins. "Man," Benjamin later wrote, "is sometimes more generous when he has little money, than when he has plenty, perhaps to prevent his being thought to have but little."

The Philadelphia waterfront in the eighteenth century, from an engraving by W. Burch and Sons, c. 1800

In 1723 Philadelphia was a sprawling, shady city of some seven thousand people. It had large grassy areas and plenty of trees. Just a few miles outside of town there were wild deer, wolves, and bears.

Most houses in Philadelphia were surrounded by trees and gardens. Stores were simply houses with a wooden beehive, anchor, crown, ship, or other symbol hanging over the door to indicate what was being sold. Inside, on the ground floor, was a room full of goods. The family lived upstairs.

When Benjamin Franklin got off the boat, he was hungry, so his first stop was a bake shop, where he bought three long puffy rolls. The pockets of his coat were stuffed with shirts and stockings, so he put one roll under each arm as he ate the third. "I made," he later wrote, "a most awkward, ridiculous appearance."

Franklin on his first day in Philadelphia buying three long puffy rolls, from a drawing by Victor A. Searles, c. 1897

On his first night in Philadelphia, Benjamin took a bed in a tavern, the Crooked Billet. The next morning he dressed as neatly as he could and went to the house of the printer Andrew Bradford. But the younger Bradford had no need for him either and sent him to Samuel Keimer, a small, strange-looking man with a long, untrimmed beard, who was setting up a print shop. Keimer hired Benjamin and found lodging for him on Market Street, at the home of Mr. and Mrs. Read.

Benjamin's days were filled with hard work. His evenings were spent talking with newfound friends, other young workingmen.

Months passed, and then Benjamin received a letter from Robert Holmes, a ship's captain who had married Benjamin's sister Mary. Holmes wrote how upset Josiah and Abiah Franklin were that Benjamin had run off and urged him to go home. Benjamin wrote back his many reasons for leaving Boston and that he intended to stay right where he was.

Excerpts from

The American Weekly Mercury

Yesterday there happened a strange accident on Board of Capt. Annis as they were unloading and getting a small box out of the Hold of the Vessel in which was Aqua Fortis one of the Bottles happened to break and set fire to the Ship which they soon got out, but the Saylor that went into the Hold to bring the box, as it was burning is since dead with the suffocating smell. There was onboard the Ship at the same Time about 150 Cask of Gun-Powder.   —June 20–27, 1723

YESTERDAY were tryed at the General Quarter Sessions for this City and County James Smith alias Spurling, and Isaac Barker alias James Stunbery, upon an Indictment for endeavouring to pass Counterfeit Bars of Gold, of which they were found Guilty, and received Sentence to stand in the Pillory for the Space of one Houre, on Saturday next, and then to be tied to a Carts-Tail, and receive 30 lashes through the Town and never to return again. We have Advice by Captain Mackey from Holland but last from Dover that Governour Shure of Boston was in a short Time to Imbark (for his Government) with 2000 Men.

—August 29–September 5, 1723

ADVERTISEMENTS
Take Notice

THERE is lately arriv'd in this city a Person who freely offers his Service to teach his poor Brethren the Male Negroes to read the Holy Scriptures, in a very uncommon, expeditious and delightful Manner, without any Manner of Expense to their respective Masters or Mistresses. All serious Persons, whether Roman Catholicks, Episcopalians, Presbyterians, Independents, Water Baptist or People called Quakers, who are truly concern'd for their Salvation, may advice with the said Person at his Lodgings (relating to the Time and Place of his so instructing them) at the Dwelling House of John Read, Carpenter in High Street, Philadelphia, every Morning till Eight of the Clock, except on the Seventh Day.

Very good English Peace, and choice good Chocolate, to be sold by Andrew Bradford, in the Second Street in Philadelphia.

All Persons who are indebted to Samuel Hackney in the High Street near the Market, are desired to come and pay the same; and those to whom he is indebted are desired to bring in their Accounts in order to be adjusted by reason he designs to leave this City of Philadelphia and depart for Great Britain in about six weeks time.

—February 5–12, 1723

To be Sold, Three very Likely Negro Girls being about 16 Years of age, and a Negro Boy about 14, all speaking good English, enquire of the Printer hereof.

At the House of Henry Clifton Starch-Maker in the Third Street in Philadelphia, is to be sold, good white Starch at One Pound Fifteen Shillings, per Hundred, and at four Shillings per Dozen, and five Pence the single Pound.

Run away from Joseph Colemen in the Great Valley, a Negro Man named Tom, formerly belonging to Capt. Palmer, aged about 30 Years, of a Middle Stature, and a flat Nose, he has Stockings and Shoes on, a white Shirt and an old Hat, and a blue girdle round his Waist, talks good English. Whosoever takes up the said Negro and puts him into Philadelphia Gaol, shall have 20 Shillings Reward.

—June 13–19, 1723

The American Weekly Mercury, *Philadelphia's first newspaper, began publication on December 22, 1719. These selections are all from 1723, the year of Franklin's arrival in that city. Among the major stories in the paper that year was a serialized abstract of a sermon "against the Inoculation of the Small Pox" given by Mr. Massey, who the* Weekly Mercury *reported "seems privy to the Devil's Designs."*

Benjamin Franklin talking to Governor Keith, from a drawing by Victor A. Searles, c. 1897

Holmes showed Benjamin's well-written letter to his friend Sir William Keith, the governor of Pennsylvania. Sir William was impressed with it, especially when he was told the writer was just eighteen. Some time later, he stopped by Keimer's print shop and invited Benjamin to join him for some wine at a nearby tavern. There he offered to help Benjamin set up his own shop, give him colony business, and do everything he could to make him a success.

Now Benjamin was ready to go home.

The trip from Philadelphia took two weeks. No one knew he was coming, so his arrival in Boston was a pleasant surprise to everyone in his family—everyone but James.

Benjamin went to his brother's print shop, surely to show how well he was doing. He wore fine clothes and showed off his new watch and pocketful of silver coins. James looked at Benjamin coldly, then turned and went back to work. James was not interested in his younger brother or in his success. Mrs. Franklin tried to reconcile her two sons, but James would have none of it.

Benjamin proudly showed his father a letter from Sir William outlining the governor's great plans for the boy. Benjamin asked his father for money to buy a press and type. Josiah Franklin thought about it, but decided Benjamin was too young to start his own business. He told his disappointed son to return to Philadelphia, work hard, and save his money. If by the time he was twenty-one he felt ready to set up shop, then he would help him.

Benjamin returned to Philadelphia.

"Your father is too prudent," Sir William told him. "Since he will not set you up, I will do it myself." He told Benjamin to go to London and use letters of credit he would give him to buy paper, type, and a printing press.

Benjamin was excited at the prospect of owning his own business, but he kept his plans secret, even from his closest friends. He continued to work in Keimer's print shop during his wait of several months to sail to London. He continued, too, to live with the Reads. And he courted their eighteen-year-old daughter—lively, handsome, and sometimes sharp-tongued Deborah Read. "I had great Respect and Affection for her," Franklin wrote later in his autobiography, "and had some Reason to believe she had the same for me."

Benjamin wanted to marry Deborah. Her father had just died, so Benjamin spoke to Mrs. Read. He told her his plan and she told him he was too young to be married. Besides, he was about to take a long journey. Mrs. Read advised him to wait until he returned.

Benjamin Franklin left Philadelphia on November 10, 1724, aboard the *London-Hope*. Six weeks later, on December 24, he arrived in London. He was told the promised letters of credit were in a bag from Sir William. Just before the ship docked, the bag was opened. There were no letters for Benjamin Franklin.

Benjamin told Thomas Denham, a Quaker merchant who had sailed with him, about the missing letters. "He let me into Keith's character," Franklin later wrote. "No one who knew him had the smallest dependence on him; and he laughed at the Governor's giving me a letter of credit, having, he said, no credit to give."

Eighteen-year-old Benjamin Franklin was in the great city of London all alone and almost penniless.

London was unlike any place Benjamin Franklin had ever seen in the American colonies. It was then a city of more than 600,000 people, the largest city in western Europe. It had theaters, churches, fashionable-clothing and silversmith shops, markets, coffeehouses, inns, and taverns. It was a busy, noisy, sometimes dangerous city. Stories of mail coach robberies and murders filled London newspapers. Game birds and silver were even stolen from the king's castle.

Denham advised Benjamin Franklin to take a job with one of the more than seventy-five master printers in London. "I immediately got into work at Palmer's, then a famous printing-house . . . and here I continued near a year."

At Palmer's, Benjamin marveled at the beer-drinking habits of his fellow workers. "My companion at the press," Franklin later wrote, "drank every day a pint before breakfast, a pint at breakfast with his bread and cheese, a pint between breakfast and dinner, a pint at dinner, a pint in the

A view of eighteenth-century London, from a print by Bowles, c. 1752

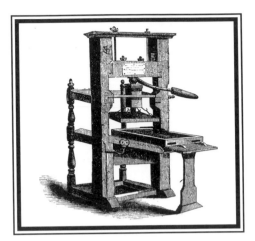

The press Franklin worked on
at the Watts Print Shop in London,
from an engraving, c. 1850

Benjamin Franklin at twenty, from an engraving
by H. B. Hall, c. 1860, based on a painting by
Robert Feke, said to have been done in London
in 1726. Some historians question
if it is Franklin. They wonder how a young
man working for meager wages could have
afforded such expensive clothes and
have paid for a portrait.

afternoon about six o'clock, and another when he had done his day's work." That's six pints of beer—strong beer. The Englishmen felt strong English beer would make them strong enough to do hard work.

Benjamin Franklin drank only water. His coworkers called him the "Water-American," but Benjamin Franklin was the strong one. "I carried up and down stairs a large form of types in each hand," he wrote, "when others carried but one in both hands."

Franklin enjoyed his time in London. He went to plays and concerts and found a great many books to read. He even wrote a philosophical booklet of his own, "A Dissertation on Liberty and Necessity, Pleasure and Pain."

After about a year at Palmer's, he worked at Watts's, "a still greater printing house." There he met Wygate, an "ingenious young man" with "wealthy relations." Benjamin Franklin taught him how to swim. Then Franklin "stripped and leaped into the river, and swam from near Chelsea to Blackfriars," a distance of four miles, "performing on the way many feats of activity, both upon and under water."

Wygate was impressed. He proposed that he and Benjamin travel together across Europe and teach swimming. "I was once inclined to it," Franklin wrote. He spoke about it with his friend Mr. Denham. "Think only of returning to Pennsylvania," Denham advised. Then he offered Benjamin a job as the chief clerk in a store he planned to open in Philadelphia.

Franklin happily accepted and left the printing business, he thought forever.

Benjamin Franklin worked in London for Denham, buying goods, having them prepared for shipment, and running errands. Then, on July 22, 1726, Franklin and Denham began an almost three-month sea journey home.

On the ship, Franklin had plenty of time to think, to form "a regular design" for his life. He resolved to be frugal, hardworking, honest, and "speak ill of no man whatever . . . and on proper occasions speak all the good I know of everybody."

Franklin kept a shipboard diary, too. He wrote in it of birds, dolphins, flying fish, sharks, seaweed, and whatever else caught his eye. He also wrote of a fellow passenger caught cheating at cards: "With much struggling," Franklin and some others on the boat tied a rope "fast about his middle and hoisted him up into the air. . . . We let him hang, cursing and swearing, for nearly a quarter of an hour." Then the card cheat's fellow passengers did not "play, eat, drink, or converse with him" for five days, until the card cheat paid a fine of two bottles of brandy. "Man," Franklin wrote of the incident, "is a sociable being . . . one of the worst of punishments [is] to be excluded from society."

By October 7, 1726, Franklin had been at sea for almost eighty days. He was afraid that perhaps he would never get home. He wrote in his diary, "Sure the American continent is not sunk under water since we left it."

Two days later someone aboard "pronounced the long wished-for sound: LAND! LAND!" Within the hour others saw the tops of trees. But not Franklin. "I could not discern it so soon as the rest; my eyes were dimmed with the suffusion of two small drops of joy."

5.

THE BUSY BODY

In the time Benjamin Franklin had been away, Philadelphia had grown. People had moved there from outlying areas and from abroad. New houses and shops had been built. There was lots of talk of money, the need to make it and to save it.

Franklin quickly kept his resolution to be hardworking. He worked untiringly in Mr. Denham's store as a salesman and bookkeeper. He lived with Denham, too.

"He counseled me as a father," Franklin wrote of Denham, "having a sincere regard for me. I respected and loved him."

Then, in February 1727, after just four months in the store, both he and Mr. Denham became very sick. "My distemper," Franklin later wrote, "was a pleurisy, which very nearly carried me off. I suffered a good deal."

Benjamin Franklin survived the illness, but Denham didn't. "It held him a long time," Franklin wrote, "and at length carried him off. . . . He left me once more to the wide World; for the Store was taken into the Care of his Executors, and my Employment under him ended."

Franklin's hard work in London and for Denham had sadly brought him back to where he started in Philadephia. He returned to Keimer's print shop. He took a job there as foreman.

Keimer had five workers whom Franklin described as "raw, cheap hands." Franklin knew the plan was to have him train the men and then to let him go. "I went on, however, very cheerfully, put his printing-house in order, which had been in great confusion. . . . I was warehouse-man and everything . . . but however serviceable I might be, I found that my services became every day of less importance as the other hands improved in the business."

Keimer became more the boss and often found fault with Franklin. Keimer complained about the high wages he was paying him. "At length," Franklin wrote, "a trifle snapped our connections."

There was a loud noise outside the shop. Franklin put his head out the window and Keimer, "being in the street, looked up and saw me, called out to me in a loud and angry tone to mind my business." Keimer rushed inside. "High words passed on both sides," and Keimer told Franklin he would keep him until the end of the quarter, but no longer.

Franklin was too proud to stay even that long. He quit.

Hugh Meredith, who worked with Franklin, — "bred to country work; honest, sensible," by Franklin's description, "something of a reader, but given to drink"—convinced his father to set the two young men in business, so in 1728 Benjamin Franklin and Hugh Meredith became partners in a new print shop. Meredith supplied the money and Franklin did most of the work.

Benjamin Franklin had secret plans to make his print shop a success. One day, to his regret, he confided them to a stranger.

George Webb, who had worked with Franklin at Keimer's, came look-ing for a job. Franklin said he had nothing at the moment, but expected to have work for him soon. Then he told his secret. There was just one news-paper in Philadelphia, Bradford's *American Weekly Mercury*, which was filled with six-month-old news from Europe. Franklin told Webb his ideas for a more interesting newspaper. And he told Webb that when he was ready to start printing it, there would be work for him.

"None are deceived but they that confide," Benjamin Franklin later wrote in an almanac, and Franklin was deceived.

Webb went straight to Keimer and told him Franklin's plans. Keimer quickly started his own weekly newspaper, the *Universal Instructor in all Arts and Sciences, and Pennsylvania Gazette.*

"The sleeping Fox catches no poultry," Benjamin Franklin also wrote in an almanac, and Franklin was surely no sleeping fox. He wrote a series of letters with some of the same humor of his earlier Silence Dogood pieces. He signed them, "Your most humble Servant, *The Busy Body.*" He sent the letters to the *American Weekly Mercury,* with the hope they would help that paper at the expense of Keimer's.

Franklin's plan worked. His letters helped boost the circulation of the *American Weekly Mercury* and Keimer's newspaper lost readers. After nine months, with just ninety subscribers, Keimer was bankrupt. He sold his newspaper to Franklin and Meredith and moved to Barbados.

Franklin shortened the name of the newspaper to the *Pennsylvania Gazette.* He became both the writer and editor of the paper and promised to make it "as agreeable and useful an entertainment as the nature of the thing will allow."

The newspaper was well written, even if sometimes in a light-hearted manner. When a farmer was struck by lightning and survived, except for a pewter button on his pants that had melted, Franklin wrote, "Tis well nothing else thereabouts was made of pewter." When there were no letters to the editor of real interest, Franklin wrote some to himself and answered them. He was the first to publish a newspaper cartoon and a map to illustrate a news story. The *Pennsylvania Gazette* soon became the best newspaper published in the American colonies.

The newspaper prospered, but Franklin's partnership with Meredith

Front page of Franklin and Meredith's first issue of the Pennsylvania Gazette.

didn't. Meredith, who was often drunk, decided he wasn't meant to be a printer. He was meant to be a farmer. Franklin borrowed money from two friends, paid the shop's and Meredith's debts, and the business was all his.

Franklin sold paper, parchment, ink, lampblack, legal forms, and peddler's sales books in his shop. He printed money for the Delaware colony. "For the industry of that Franklin," said one of his neighbors, "is superior to anything I ever saw of the kind." Franklin was not only industrious, but he made sure the people of Philadelphia knew it. He dressed plainly and was careful not to be seen standing about and talking. Sometimes, to show that he was not above doing any of the work

Benjamin Franklin at work, from a drawing by Victor A. Searles, c. 1897

Deborah Read Franklin, from a portrait by Matthew Pratt, surely based on a similar one by Benjamin Wilson, c. 1766

necessary for his shop, he pushed a wheelbarrow piled high with paper through the streets of Philadelphia.

With his work life improving, Franklin's thoughts turned to marriage.

In 1726, when Franklin returned to Philadelphia, "Keith was no longer governor," Franklin wrote in his autobiography. "I met him walking the streets as a common citizen. He seem'd a little asham'd at seeing me, but passed without saying any thing." Franklin added, "I should have been as much asham'd at seeing Miss Read."

In 1724, before he sailed to London, Franklin had promised to marry Deborah Read. But all the time he was away, Franklin had written just one letter to her. By the time he returned, she was married to someone else, a potter named Rogers.

Deborah was miserable with the potter. She suspected he had another wife and she soon moved back with her mother. A year later, Rogers ran off to the West Indies, to escape the many people he owed money. Soon there were rumors that he died.

"Our mutual affection was revived," Franklin wrote of Deborah Read, "and I took her to wife September 1st, 1730."

Deborah Read Franklin was a kind woman. She was helpful, industrious, thrifty, and capable. She helped Benjamin Franklin in his work and made his clothes. "It was a comfort to me," Franklin once wrote to Deborah, "to recollect that I had once been clothed from head to foot in woolen and linen of my wife's manufacture, and that I had never been prouder of any dress in my life."

Sometime in 1730 or early 1731, Benjamin Franklin had a son. The child, William, a future royal governor of New Jersey, was conceived before Franklin married, and the boy's mother was not Deborah Read.

"That hard-to-be-govern'd Passion of Youth," Franklin wrote in his autobiography, "hurried me frequently into Intrigues with low Women." Perhaps one of those women was William Franklin's mother. The boy was raised in the Franklin household by Benjamin and Deborah.

In 1732 Benjamin and Deborah Franklin had a son together, Francis Folger Franklin. Four years later, in 1736, a smallpox epidemic spread across Philadelphia. Visitors to the city fled. But the Franklins remained and sweet, lively, four-year-old Francis was stricken with smallpox. He soon died.

"The delight of all that knew him," Franklin had etched on his son's tombstone. And thirty-six years later when talking of a grandson, Franklin remembered Francis, "whom to this day," he said, "I cannot think of without a sigh."

People in Philadelphia blamed Franklin for his son's death, saying that the boy got the disease from a smallpox inoculation. Benjamin Franklin answered them.

"I do hereby sincerely declare," Franklin stated in the *Pennsylvania Gazette*, "that he was not inoculated, but receiv'd the Distemper in the common Way of Infection. And I suppose the Report could only arise from its being my known Opinion, that inoculation

William Franklin, from an etching by Albert Rosenthal, based on a painting by Mather Brown, c. 1790

Francis Folger Franklin, from an engraving by H. B. Hall, c. 1860

was a safe and beneficial Practice." He wrote in that same notice, surely with great regret, "I intended to have my Child inoculated, as soon as he shou'd have recovered sufficient Strength from the Flux with which he had been long afflicted."

In 1743 Deborah Franklin gave birth to a girl, named Sarah but known as Sally.

"Sally grows a fine girl, and is extremely industrious with her needle, and delights in her work," Benjamin Franklin wrote in a 1751 letter to his sister Jane Mecom. "I have hopes that she will prove an ingenious, sensible, notable, and worthy woman." He praised her for having "the best Natural Disposition in the World."

Franklin was also proud of Sally's love of reading. In a letter to his mother he wrote, "Your granddaughter is the greatest lover of her book and school of any child I ever knew."

Sally was devoted to her parents. She and her mother went together to church. She and her father went riding together. In 1763 they rode on a sixteen-hundred-mile tour of post offices. Sally was a good and cheerful daughter, but by the time she was in her twenties, Franklin worried she might never get married. "My dear Papa likes to hear of weddings," Sally teased him in a 1765 letter, and she listed for her father her many friends who had recently married.

Sarah Franklin Bache, from an engraving by H. B. Hall, c. 1860, more flattering than the 1791 painting by John Hoppner on which it was based, that showed a less glamorous woman, with more rugged features and a greater resemblance to her father

Soon Sally would marry, too.

In 1766 Sally's best friend, Peggy Ross, was engaged to be married to Richard Bache, a shipowner and trader. But Peggy suffered from a long and lingering sickness and, according to one of his granddaughters, when Peggy was near death she asked Richard to marry her friend Sally Franklin. He did. They married in October 1767.

"I can only say," Franklin wrote at the time, "if he proves a good husband to her, and a good son to me, he shall find me as good a father as I can be."

Sally and Richard Bache had eight children: Benjamin, William, Sarah who died before her first birthday, Elizabeth, Louis, Deborah, Richard, and another Sarah.

Franklin's first child, William, had children, too. And just like his father, he had his first child, a son named William Temple, before he married. There is also no record of who that boy's mother was. William later married Elizabeth Downes and they had a daughter, Ellen.

Among Franklin's grandchildren and great-grandchildren were many clergymen, physicians, and army and naval officers. In a bit of irony, while Benjamin Franklin was a great American patriot, his grandson Richard Bache was the only member of the Texas Senate in 1845 to vote against union with the United States.

6.

FIRST CITIZEN OF PHILADELPHIA

"Can a man arrive at perfection in his life?"

"Which is best, to make a friend of a wise and good man that is poor, or of a rich man that is neither wise nor good?"

"Does it not require as much pains, study, and application, to become truly wise and strictly virtuous, as to become rich?" "Which of the two is happiest in life?"

"Can any one particular form of government suit all mankind?"

"Why does the flame of a candle tend upward in a spire?"

"Whence comes the dew, that stands on the outside of a tankard that has cold water in it in the summer time?"

These and many other questions were discussed on Friday evenings at the Junto, a club formed in 1727 by Benjamin Franklin and several of his Philadelphia friends. The purpose of the club was to improve its members and fellow citizens in virtue, knowledge, and practical wisdom. On joining, each member had to declare he loved mankind in general and truth for truth's sake.

It was a private club. "We had from the beginning made it a rule to keep our institution a secret," Franklin later wrote. "The intention was to avoid applications of improper persons for admittance."

Franklin loved the Junto. Almost fifty years after it was formed, he wrote to a fellow member, "Since we have held that Club till we are grown gray together, let us hold it out to the end. . . . I love company . . . I therefore hope it will not be discontinued as long as we are able to crawl together." According to Franklin, the Junto "was the best school of philosophy, morality, and politics that then existed in the Province."

During the early days of the Junto, members often brought books along to help with whatever debate was planned for the night. Franklin suggested that the members keep all their books in the Junto room and share them. The plan was approved and one end of the room became the club library.

Books were expensive then, and many came from overseas. When some books in the Junto library were damaged, their owners took them home and there was no more library. Benjamin Franklin fixed that. Early in 1731 he proposed a subscription library. Members would pay to join, for the first purchase of books, and then pay a yearly fee to add to the library's collection.

Franklin's subscription library, from a painting by Charles E. Mills, c. 1910

COPR. DETROIT PUBLISHING CO.

By November 1731, fifty people had agreed to join Franklin's Library Company of Philadelphia, the first subscription library in America. By October 1732 the first books arrived from London, and surely one of the happiest patrons of the library was Benjamin Franklin. Now, with many books available to him, he set aside an hour or two each day to read.

There was more to be done in Philadelphia, and Benjamin Franklin went about doing it.

Electrical storms during the hot summer of 1734 caused many fires. Once a fire started, the mostly wood buildings just kept burning. Franklin wrote a paper on the problem and read it to the Junto. Then he sent an unsigned letter to his own newspaper, the *Pennsylvania Gazette*. (It seems he seldom signed his name to letters he wrote to newspapers!) In his letter were hints to avoid causing fires, and his proposal for a fire-fighting club. With his help, in 1736, the Union Fire Company, Philadelphia's first fire department, was formed.

Next, Franklin worked on improving the Philadelphia police department, then called the city watch. There was one constable for each area, who along with six homeowners would walk about to be sure every home, every citizen, was safe. If a homeowner didn't want to take his turn, he could pay six shillings a year to hire a substitute. Franklin found that usually no substitute was hired. The six shillings ended up in the constable's pocket. And the constable didn't walk the rounds, either. Most of his nights were spent in tippling—whiskey drinking.

Franklin proposed to tax homeowners according to the value of their property and use the money to hire a full-time police force. He presented his idea at the Junto. He wrote about the problem in the *Gazette*. It took some time, but Franklin's ideas were adopted.

In October 1736 civic-minded Benjamin Franklin was appointed clerk of the Pennsylvania Assembly. This job came with its own rewards. It brought him government printing work.

The next year, a new member of the Assembly wanted to give the clerk job to someone else and Franklin tested the maxim, "He that has once done you a kindness will be more ready to do you another than he whom you yourself have obliged." Franklin had the new member "do him a kindness." Franklin borrowed a rare book from the man, talked to him about it, won the man over, and kept his job as clerk.

In August 1751 Benjamin Franklin became a member of the Assembly, elected to represent the people of Philadelphia. His son, William, then twenty years old, was made clerk.

In 1737 Benjamin Franklin was made Deputy Postmaster of Philadelphia and in 1753 Deputy Postmaster General for all the northern colonies. The man appointed for the southern colonies was often sick, so Franklin did his job, too.

In those days, people came to the post office to pick up and pay for their mail. In Philadelphia, Franklin started a system of home delivery. If someone didn't come for a letter, Franklin had it brought to his door for an added charge. The man who delivered the letters and collected the pennies was called the penny postman. Franklin also set up America's first Dead Letter Office for letters left unclaimed after three months.

In colonial America, it was the right of the postmaster to keep his riders from carrying certain newspapers. When Andrew Bradford was postmaster, he only allowed delivery of his newspaper, the *American Weekly Mercury.* "I thought so meanly of the practice," Franklin wrote, "that when I afterwards came into his situation, I took care never to imitate it."

Philadelphia was nicknamed "Filthy-dirty" by some farmers' wives because its streets were unpaved, and when it rained, people walked about in mud. Benjamin Franklin helped get the streets paved and hired a man to keep the pavement clean.

In the mid-1740s a war was on in America, King George's War, one of the French and Indian wars between France and England. Pennsylvania had no army and no cannons to defend the busy port of Philadelphia. What if Philadelphia was attacked?

"On the first alarm, terror will spread over all," Franklin wrote in 1747 in *Plain Truth*, a pamphlet that urged that an army be formed. "All will run into confusion, amidst cries and lamentations. . . . Sacking the city will be the first, and burning it, in all probability, the last act of the enemy. . . . A dreadful scene!"

A few days after he distributed *Plain Truth*, Franklin called a meeting and twelve hundred men joined an Association for Defense. Within a few days, more than ten thousand had joined. Pennsylvania had its army.

And what about the young people?

Franklin wrote another pamphlet, *Proposals relating to the Education of Youth in Pennsylvania*. He proposed a school to teach "a fair, swift hand-writing, arithmetic, book-keeping, the rudiments of geometry and astronomy, the English language,

The cover of Plain Truth,
*the pamphlet Franklin wrote and
printed that encouraged the people
of eastern Pennsylvania to
form an Association for Defense*

PLAIN TRUTH:
Ses. Thor. Mason
OR,

SERIOUS CONSIDERATIONS

On the PRESENT STATE of the

CITY of *PHILADELPHIA*,

AND

PROVINCE of *PENNSYLVANIA*.

By a TRADESMAN of *Philadelphia*.
viz. — Benjamin Franklin Pel.

Capta urbe, nibil fit reliqui victis. Sed, per Deos immortales, vos ego appello, qui semper domos, villas, signa, tabulas vestras, tantæ æstimationis fecistis; si ista, cujuscumque modi sint, quæ amplexamini, retinere, si voluptatibus vestris otium præbere vultis; expergiscimini aliquando, & capessite rempublicam. Non agitur nunc de sociorum injuriis; LIBERTAS & ANIMA *nostra in dubio est. Dux hostium cum exercitu supra caput est. Vos cunctamini etiam nunc, & dubitatis quid faciatis? Scilicet, res ipsa aspera est, sed vos non timetis eam. Imo vero maxume; sed inertiâ & mollitiâ animi, alius alium exspectantes, cunctamini; videlicet, Diis immortalibus confisi, qui hanc rempublicam in maximis periculis servavere.* NON VOTIS, NEQUE SUPPLICIIS MULIEBRIBUS, AUXILIA DEORUM PARANTUR: *vigilando, agendo, bene consulendo, prospere omnia cedunt. Ubi socordiæ tete atque ignaviæ tradideris, nequicquam Deos implores; irati, infestique sunt.* M. POR. CAT. *in* SALUST.

Printed in the YEAR MDCCXLVII.

geography, history, logic, natural science, good morals, and good manners." Money was collected and in 1751 Franklin had his school, the Academy of Philadelphia. It later became the University of Pennsylvania.

"There is no such thing," Dr. Thomas Bond told Benjamin Franklin, "as carrying through a public-spirited project without you are concerned in it." So when Dr. Bond wanted to start a hospital, he asked Franklin to help him.

Benjamin Franklin wrote about the need for a hospital in two issues of the *Gazette.* Many people, including Franklin himself, contributed money to the project, but not enough, so Franklin proposed that the Pennsylvania Assembly match contributions collected from individuals. Franklin's fellow members of the Assembly agreed, and the hospital was built. It "Was piously founded," Franklin wrote in 1755 for the hospital cornerstone, "For the relief of the sick and miserable; May the God of Mercies Bless the Undertaking."

Even earlier, in May 1743, Franklin sent a letter to his learned friends and proposed they meet and correspond on a long list of subjects, including new developments in agriculture, medicine, geology, archaeology, mathematics, chemistry, animal husbandry, "and all philosophical experiments that let light into the nature of things, tend to increase the power of man over matter, and multiply the conveniences or pleasures of life." The list was surely a reflection of Franklin's ever curious mind. That letter led to the formation of the American Philosophical Society.

There seemed no limit to Franklin's interests and the ways he improved the lives of his neighbors. He truly was the First Citizen of Philadelphia.

7.

POOR RICHARD

In Franklin's time, there were two books in just about every colonial home, a Bible and an almanac. The Bible helped guide people's religious lives. The almanac helped with almost everything else.

Almanacs then were complete calendars, noting holidays, seasons, dates of fairs and when courts were open, times of sunrise and sunset, the tides, phases of the moon, and eclipses. They were filled with other information, too, and predictions of the weather. House-to-house peddlers carried them along with their other offerings—pins, needles, thread, mirrors, and pots. If someone didn't have the money to buy an almanac, he might pay with a sack of potatoes or a bundle of wheat.

Franklin imported copies of *Poor Robin's Almanac* from England and sold them in his shop. From 1729 to 1732, he published almanacs by Thomas Godfrey and John Jerman. Then, in December 1732, Franklin announced in his newspaper, the *Pennsylvania Gazette,* a new almanac.

Just published for 1733: POOR RICHARD: An ALMANACK containing Lunations, Eclipses, Planets Motions and Aspects,

Weather Sun and Moon's Rising and Setting, Highwater, etc, beside many pleasant and witty Verses, Jests, and Sayings, Author's Motive of Writing, Prediction of the Death of his Friend Mr. Titan Leeds, Moon no Cuckold, Batchelor's Folly, Parson's Wine and Baker's Pudding, Short Visits, Kings and Bears, New Fashions, Game for Kisses, Katherine's Love, Different Sentiments, Signs of a Tempest, Death of a Fisherman, Conjugal Debate, Men and Melons, H. the Prodigal, Breakfast in Bed, Oyster lawsuit, etc. By Richard SAUNDERS, Philomat. Printed and Sold by B. Franklin. Price 3s 6d per dozen.

"The plain truth of the matter is," Richard Saunders wrote in the preface to the 1733 almanac, to explain why he had written it, "I am excessive poor, and my wife, good woman, is, I tell her, excessive proud... and has threatened more than once to burn all my books and rattling-traps, (as she calls my instruments,) if I do not make some profitable use of them for the good of my family. The printer has offer'd me some considerable share of the profits, and I have thus begun to comply with my dame's desire."

The printer, of course, was Benjamin Franklin. He was the writer, too—Richard Saunders.

To stir up interest in the first *Poor Richard's Almanack*, Franklin predicted the death of Titan Leeds, until then the author of the most popular of the Philadelphia almanacs. "He dies," Franklin wrote, "by my calculation, made at his request, on October 17, 1733, 3 ho., 29 m., P.M."

The cover of Franklin's first almanac

Poor Richard, 1733.

AN

Almanack

For the Year of Chrift

1733,

Being the Firft after LEAP YEAR:

And makes fince the Creation	Years
By the Account of the Eaftern *Greeks*	7241
By the Latin Church, when ☉ ent. ♈	6932
By the Computation of *W.W.*	5742
By the *Roman* Chronology	5682
By the *Jewifh* Rabbies	5494

Wherein is contained

The Lunations, Eclipfes, Judgment of the Weather, Spring Tides, Planets Motions & mutual Afpeêts, Sun and Moon's Rifing and Setting, Length of Days, Time of High Water, Falls, Courts, and obfervable Days Fitted to the Latitude of Forty Degrees, and a Meridian of Five Hours Weft from *London*, but may without fenfible Error, ferve all the adjacent Places, even from *Newfoundland* to *South-Carolina*.

By *RICHARD SAUNDERS*, Philom.

PHILADELPHIA:
Printed and fold by *B. FRANKLIN*, at the New Printing Office near the Market.

The Third Impreffion.

Of the DISEASES this Year

THIS Year the Stone-blind shall see but very little; the Deaf shall hear poorly, and the Dumb shan't speak very plain. And it's much, if my Dame *Bridget* talks at all this Year. Whole Flocks, Herds and Droves of Sheep, Swine and Oxen, Cocks and Hens, Ducks and Drakes, Geese and Ganders shall go to Pot; the Mortality will not be altogether so great among Cats, Dogs and Horses. As for old Age, 'twill be incurable this Year, because of the Years past. And towards the Fall some People will be seized with an unaccountable Inclination to roast and eat their own Ears: Should this be call'd Madness, Doctors? I think not. ---- But the worst Disease of all will be a certain most horrid, dreadful, malignant, catching, perverse and odious Malady, almost epidemical, insomuch that many shall run Mad upon it; I quake for very Fear when I think on't; For I assure you very few will escape the Disease, which is called by the learned Albumazar *Lack o'mony.*   ——1739

—Pay what you owe,
  and what you're worth you'll know.
—Clean your finger, before you point
  at my spots.

—You may be too cunning For One,
  but not for All.
—You can bear your own Faults,
  and Why not a Fault in your Wife.
—The Golden Age never was the present
  Age.
—Genius without Education
  is like Silver in the Mine.   ——1750

For the Ague or Intermitting Fever

Take one Ounce of good *Peruvian* Bark, finely levigaated; make it into an Electuary with Treaciel or Melosses, mixing therewith twenty or thirty Drops of Laudanum; take this at about six or eight Doses two or three Hours apart, washing it down with a Glass of Madeira or red Wine. If any thing like the Jaundice, or Yellow-ness about the Eyes remains, chew Rhubarb a few Mornings.

For the Dry-Gripes

Take sixty Drops of Tincture of Castor, thirty of liquid Laudanum, in an ounce of mint or other simple Water, sweetened to your Taste; take of this mixture a Spoonful every Half Hour, till you find Relief.

These Remedies are said to be excellent in their Kind; but as a Case may be mistaken by the unskilful, let me, tho' no Physician, prescribe something more, *wiz.* Whenever you can have the Advice of a skilful Physician, *Take that.*

          ——1756

The Benefit of going to LAW

Two Beggars traveling along,
  One blind, the other lame,
Pick'd up an Oyster on the Way
  To which they both laid claim:
The Matter rose so high, that they
  Resolv'd to go to Law,
As often richer Fools have done
  Who quarrel for a Straw.
A Lawyer took it straight in hand,
  Who knew his business was,
To mind nor one nor t'other side,
  But make the best o'th Cause
As always in the Law's the Case:
  So he his Judgment gave.
And Lawyer-like he thus resolv'd
  What each of them should have:
Blind Plaintiff, lame defendant share
The Friendly Laws impartial Care
A Shell For him, a Shell For thee
The Middle is the Lawyer's Fee
          ——1733.

Titan Leeds was furious. He called Poor Richard Saunders "a false predictor, an ignorant, conceited scribbler, a fool and a liar," and insisted he would still be writing his almanac long after Saunders was dead.

In his 1734 almanac Franklin admitted he was not a witness at Leeds's deathbed, "but there is the strongest probability that my dear friend is no more; for there appears in his name, as I am assured, an Almanack for the year 1734, in which I am treated in a very gross and unhandsome manner; in which I am called *a false Predicter, an Ignorant, a conceited Scribler, a Fool and a Lyar.* Mr. Leeds was too well bred, to use any man so indecently and so scurrilously, and moreover, his esteem and affection for me was extraordinary."

In the 1735 *Poor Richard's Almanack,* Franklin wrote that it was "the Ghost of Titan Leeds" who was writing those almanacs, for "'tis undoubtedly true that he is really defunct and dead."

Titan Leeds answered in his almanac that there was no Richard Saunders.

How could Benjamin Franklin prove that Titan Leeds was truly dead? In his 1740 almanac, he printed a letter he pretended to have received from Leeds, in which Leeds himself admitted he had died.

"They say your Prediction of my Death in 1733 was false," Franklin wrote in that phony letter, "and they pretend that I remained alive many Years after. But I hereby certify that I did actually die at that time, precisely at the Hour you men-

An inside page of Poor Richard's Almanack

tion'd, with a Variation only of 5 min. 53 sec. Which must be allow'd to be no great matter in such Cases." Franklin signed the letter, "Your affectionate Friend, T Leeds."

Of course, the Saunders-Leeds battle of words could not go on forever. It ended in the early 1740s with the real death of Titan Leeds. But it did what Franklin had hoped it would do. It brought attention to his new almanac.

Another feud in his almanacs, meant to stir interest in them, was the one between Benjamin Franklin's fictional husband and wife, Richard and Bridget Saunders.

Richard Saunders wrote of idle women in the 1733 almanac, "She that will eat breakfast in her bed, And spend the morn in dressing her head." In the next almanac, Bridget Saunders wrote of worthless men, "He that for sake of Drink neglects his Trade, And spends each Night in Taverns till 'tis late. . . . And ne'er regards his starving Family. . . ."

In 1738 Franklin claimed Bridget Saunders grabbed the almanac before it reached the printer. "I open'd it, to see if he had not been flinging some of his old Skitts at me. Just as I thought, so it was." She complained, "Cannot I have a little Fault or two, but all the Country must see it in print!" She declared her husband's preface was "not worth a printing" so she scratched it all out. She also didn't like all the bad weather Richard had predicted, so she changed that, too, and scattered in some better weather, "for the Good-Women to dry their Clothes in."

Franklin filled his almanacs with funny maxims. "Men and melons are hard to know," he wrote in his 1733 almanac. Among his other humorous maxims were "Fish and visitors smell in three days" (1736); "Make haste slowly" (1744); and "If your head is wax, don't walk in the Sun" (1749).

The playful, funny writing of Benjamin Franklin made *Poor Richard's* the comic almanac of its time. It became the best-selling book in the colonies. Almost ten thousand copies of each yearly edition from 1733 to 1757 were sold. "I reaped considerable profit from it,"

Franklin wrote in his autobiography. The almanacs made him rich.

There was a sober side to his almanacs, too, including sayings on self-improvement, such as, "Search others for their virtues, thyself for thy vices" (1738); "How few there are who have courage enough to own their Faults, or resolution enough to mend them!" (1743); and "Be at War with your Vices, at Peace with your Neighbors, and let every New-Year find you a better Man" (1755).

The sayings on self-improvement were surely based on his own experiences. Some years earlier, in about 1728, he had decided to seek "moral perfection."

Franklin wrote in his autobiography, "I wished to live without committing any fault at any time.... As I knew, or thought I knew, what was right and wrong, I did not see why I might not always do the one and avoid the other."

He made a list of thirteen virtues he planned to work on—temperance, silence, order, resolution, frugality, industry, sincerity, justice, moderation, cleanliness, tranquility, chastity, and humility. He made a small book, one page for each virtue, and kept a record of how he did. "I was surprised," he wrote, "to find myself so much fuller of faults than I had imagined; but I had the satisfaction of seeing them diminish."

Franklin, however, had real trouble with two virtues, order and humility.

In his pursuit of order, he made himself a daily schedule with time for prayer, work, meals, and sleep. Nonetheless, order was one virtue he felt eluded him. "Having an exceeding good memory," he wrote, he didn't need to put things in their place. He just remembered in which place he put them.

On his attempt to be humble, Franklin wrote, "In reality there is, perhaps, no one of our natural passions so hard to subdue as Pride. Disguise it, struggle with it, beat it down, stifle it, mortify it as much as one pleases, it is still alive, and will every now and then peep out and show itself . . . for even if I could conceive that I had completely overcome it, I should probably be proud of my humility."

In his little book, before his checklist, Franklin wrote a prayer: "O powerful Goodness! bountiful Father! merciful Guide! Increase in me that wisdom which discovers my truest interest. Strengthen my resolutions to perform what that wisdom dictates."

Franklin seldom went to church, but still, he believed in God. "I never doubted," he wrote in his autobiography, "the existence of the Deity; that he made the world and governed it by his Providence; that the most acceptable service of God was the doing good to man; that our souls are immortal; and that all crime will be punished and virtue rewarded, either here or hereafter."

With all the money Franklin earned from his newspaper and almanacs, he was able to take on new projects. He gave young printers some of the money they needed to set up shops in other colonies. Then he shared in their profits. He published *Philadelphische Zeitung*, America's first German newspaper. He also had leisure time to dabble in whatever interested him.

Franklin studied foreign languages—French, Italian, Spanish, and Latin. He wrote in his autobiography, "I soon made myself so much the master of the French as to be able to read the books with ease." But perhaps he overestimated his command of the language. In 1767, on his first trip to France, he attended a meeting of the French Academy. He didn't want to let on that he didn't understand one of the speakers, so he watched a friend. Every time she applauded, he did, too. He didn't know he was applauding the speaker's praises of their American visitor, Benjamin Franklin.

Franklin also took time to exercise, to keep himself physically fit. He lifted weights and walked at least a league (about three miles) a day, often indoors. He once wrote that he had just made 469 turns in his dining room. Despite all the exercise, by the time he was fifty, he described himself as "a fat old fellow," a "Dr. Fatsides."

Franklin took hot-water baths in a copper, slipper-shaped tub. He sat in the heel of the tub, set a book on the instep, and read immersed in water, sometimes for as long as two hours at a time.

He also enjoyed baths of another sort, air baths. In a letter to a friend, he wrote, "I rise almost every morning and sit in my chamber without any clothes whatever, half an hour or an hour, according to the season, either reading or writing." He called sitting naked "a *bracing* or *tonic* bath."

Franklin, editor and author, from a painting by Charles E. Mills, c. 1910

8.

EXPERIMENTS WITH ELECTRICITY

EXPERIMENTS

AND

OBSERVATIONS

ON

ELECTRICITY,

MADE AT

PHILADELPHIA in AMERICA,

BY

BENJAMIN FRANKLIN, L. L. D. and F. R. S.

To which are added,

LETTERS and PAPERS

ON

PHILOSOPHICAL SUBJECTS.

The Whole corrected, methodized, improved, and now first collected into one Volume,

AND

Illustrated with COPPER PLATES.

LONDON:

Printed for DAVID HENRY; and sold by FRANCIS NEWBERY, at the Corner of St. Paul's Church-Yard.

MDCCLXIX.

The cover of a 1769 pamphlet of Franklin's writings on electricity

Benjamin Franklin was ever busy and ever curious, and one of the great curiosities of his time was electricity.

For thousands of years, people knew little more about electricity than that it was produced by friction. Then, in early 1746, Pieter van Musschenbroek of Leyden, Holland, discovered that a jar, soon called the Leyden jar, half-filled with water, with one end of a wire in the water and the other at a source of friction, could store electricity. He made his discovery when his assistant, a man named Cunaeus, touched the wire and received a shock. Musschenbroek then touched the wire and was knocked to the ground. "My whole body was shaken," he wrote in a letter. "I believed that I was done for."

With the Leyden jar, electricity became a plaything. People across Europe paid traveling hucksters for the thrill of being shocked. Electrical shocks were soon touted as cure-alls for paralysis, baldness, and double chins.

In 1746 Jean Nollet, a French abbé and scientist, demonstrated electrical power to King Louis XV at the Palace of Versailles. He lined up more than a hundred French guards and directed each to hold the hand of the one beside him. Then the guards at each end of the line grabbed a wire attached to a Leyden jar. The shock traveled. The guards all jumped and the king was delighted.

In the summer of 1746, Benjamin Franklin was in Boston visiting his mother when he witnessed an electrical demonstration by Dr. Archibald Spencer, a Scottish physician. Franklin was fascinated. "I never was before engaged," he wrote later, "in any study that so totally engrossed my attention and my time."

Franklin set up a laboratory in his house, closed the door, and went to work. In his early experiments, he discovered that though a chicken could be killed with a mild shock, it took a more powerful one to kill a turkey. And the meat of a chicken or turkey killed that way was especially tender.

Once, when he was about to electrocute a turkey, he grabbed a wire with each hand. "The flash was very great," Franklin wrote in a letter to his brother John, "and the crack as loud as a pistol. . . . I then felt what I know not well how to describe, a universal blow throughout my whole body from head to foot," followed by "a violent shaking of my body, which gradually remitting, my senses as gradually returned . . . part of my hand and fingers which held the chain was left white, as though the blood had been driven out, and remained so eight or ten minutes after, feeling like dead flesh. . . . I am ashamed to have been guilty of so notorious a blunder."

"The Things which hurt, instruct," Benjamin Franklin wrote in the 1745 edition of his almanac. His carelessness also taught him that since he had survived, the force it took to kill a turkey was not enough to kill a scientist.

In September 1748, so that he could devote his time to the study of science and electricity, Benjamin Franklin sold his printing business to his foreman, David Hall. Among the terms of the sale, Franklin agreed to continue to help in the editing of the *Gazette* and *Poor Richard's Almanack*.

In 1749 the now retired Franklin wrote a paper, "Observations and Suppositions Towards Forming a New Hypothesis for Explaining the Several Phenomena of Thunder-gusts." One of the main points of his paper was the similarity of electricity and lightning.

John Lining of South Carolina, a friend of Franklin's, asked how he came to such an "out-of-the-way" idea. Franklin replied with a list of the many similarities he found with electricity and lightning. They both gave light, made a crack or noise, moved quickly, could melt metals, could be carried through metals and water, and could set things on fire.

In June 1752 Benjamin Franklin conducted an outdoor experiment to prove lightning is an electrical spark. With two cedar sticks and a silk handkerchief, he made a kite. He made it of silk instead of paper, he wrote later, "to bear the wet and wind of a thunder-gust without tearing." To the top of the kite he attached a foot-long wire to act as a lightning catcher. To the string he attached a silk ribbon and a key. He and his twenty-two-year-old son William flew the kite in the midst of a storm. They stood in an open cowshed to keep the silk ribbon and themselves dry.

Benjamin Franklin noticed some loose string threads were standing out. He touched the key and felt a small electrical shock. He had proved that lightning was electricity.

Soon after his kite experiment, ships arrived from Europe with news that a similar experiment, using suggestions Franklin had made in a paper, was conducted in France in May 1752. Thomas-François D'Alibard set an iron pole with a brass tip on a hilltop. After a storm, D'Alibard found that the pole was charged with electricity.

Now that he had proved lightning was electricity, Benjamin Franklin set about making some use of his discovery. Before the end of the year, he published instructions on protecting buildings from "mischief by thunder or lightning."

Benjamin Franklin instructed his readers to put one end of an iron rod "three or four feet in the moist ground, the other may be six or eight feet above the highest part of the building. To the upper end of the rod fasten about a foot of brass wire the size of a common knitting-needle, sharpened to a fine point. . . . A house thus furnished will not be damaged by lightning, it being attracted by the points and passing through the metal into the ground without hurting anything."

Of course, for his own home, Benjamin Franklin wasn't satisfied with a simple lightning rod. His was attached to a brass ball between two metal bells. When lightning hit the rod, sparks flew and the bells sounded.

To some church leaders Franklin's invention was an intrusion on God's power. "O!" one Boston minister wrote, "there is no getting out of the mighty Hand of God. If we think to avoid it in the air, we cannot in the

Franklin and his son, William, conducting the kite experiment, from a painting by Charles E. Mills, c. 1910

earth." He theorized that all this electrical current being driven into the ground would cause earthquakes. Nonetheless, people throughout the colonies and in Europe were quick to erect lightning rods to protect their lives and property.

Benjamin Franklin conducted other experiments and invented other useful devices. He made an iron insert that fit into a fireplace and extended out. Rather than heat coming from just the opening of the fireplace, now the three sides of the insert gave off heat. "My common

The Franklin stove, from a drawing, c. 1915

room," he wrote, "is made twice as warm as it used to be, with a quarter of the wood." He called his invention the Pennsylvania fireplace. Most everyone else called it the Franklin stove.

Benjamin Franklin did not profit from his discoveries and inventions. But others did.

Franklin wrote in his autobiography that an ironworker in London "got a patent for it there, and made, as I was told, a little fortune by it." There were others who took out patents for Benjamin Franklin's inventions and he never protested, "as having no desire of profiting by patents myself and hating disputes." He further explained, "That, as we enjoy great advantages from the inventions of others, we should be glad of an opportunity to serve others by any invention of ours; and this we should do freely and generously."

In 1748 the ever curious Benjamin Franklin hung a clay pot filled with molasses by a string attached to a nail in his ceiling. In the pot he also put a single ant. The ant climbed the string to the ceiling and then down the wall. A short while later a parade of ants found their way to the molasses, because, Franklin was sure, the first ant communicated with the others.

52	61	4	13	20	29	36	45
14	3	62	51	46	35	30	19
53	60	5	12	21	28	37	44
11	6	59	54	43	38	27	22
55	58	7	10	23	26	39	42
9	8	57	56	41	40	25	24
50	63	2	15	18	31	34	47
16	1	64	49	48	33	32	17

One of Franklin's magic squares. In this one, each straight row, horizontal or vertical, added together is 260. Half of each row, beginning from an outer edge, makes 130.

Franklin invented bifocal eyeglasses, made a chair with a seat that folded to become a stepladder, and a long arm-pole that could grab things from high shelves. He also invented the armonica, an adapted form of musical glasses sometimes called the "glass harmonica." He studied sun spots, magnetism, and the common cold. He made magic squares—large squares subdivided into smaller ones, each with a different number inside. The magic happened when someone added the numbers in any horizontal, or vertical, and sometimes diagonal row. The totals were all the same.

Benjamin Franklin was honored for his scientific work. He was awarded honorary degrees from Harvard College, Yale College, and the College of William and Mary. He was elected to the French Academy of Sciences and given the Sir Godfrey Copley gold medal from the Royal Society of London "on account of his curious experiments and observations on electricity." Because of these and other honors and honorary degrees, many people began calling him Dr. Franklin.

Benjamin Franklin was never one to boast of his achievements. An English friend wrote to him, praised his work, and ended his letter with, "I think now I have stuck a Feather in thy Cap, I may be allowed to conclude in wishing thee long to wear it." Benjamin Franklin's response was a modest one. "I fear I have not so much Reason to be proud," he wrote, "for a Feather in the Cap is not so useful a Thing."

Franklin in his workshop, from a portrait by Mason Chamberlin, c. 1770

9.

GENERAL FRANKLIN

In 1754 there was war in the American colonies between France and England, one of the French and Indian Wars. The French were moving from their posts in Canada into the Ohio valley and building forts there. They were threatening to take the western frontiers of some of the colonies, including Pennsylvania.

"They presume that they may with Impunity violate the most solemn Treaties," Benjamin Franklin wrote of the French in the *Pennsylvania Gazette*, "murder and scalp our Farmers, with their Wives and Children, and take an easy Possession of such Parts of the British Territory as they find most convenient for them."

The French, a worried Benjamin Franklin wrote, were better prepared to fight. They were "under one Direction, with one Council, and one Purse." The colonies had "so many different Governments and Assemblies," too many to be able to work together quickly enough "for our common Defence and Security."

Alongside his article was perhaps the first political cartoon in America, a drawing of a snake cut into eight pieces. Beneath the snake was the warning, "JOIN, or DIE."

In June 1754 leaders of seven colonies met in Albany, New York, to deal with this crisis. Benjamin Franklin, then a member of the Pennsylvania Assembly, went to represent Pennsylvania. There he proposed that the colonies band together "for defence and other general purposes."

Franklin's plan called for a governor general, a grand council with representatives from each of the colonies, and a general treasury funded by a tax "such as may be collected with the least inconvenience to the people." The plan was approved by the congress, but the colonial governors were not willing to give up power. None of them approved Franklin's plan, not even the governor of Pennsylvania.

In the late fall of 1754, Deputy Postmaster Franklin went on a tour of post offices. When he arrived in Boston, he visited with relatives and old friends, and made many new ones. He also met with Governor William Shirley of Massachusetts.

Governor Shirley showed Franklin a proposal that had just reached him, an English plan for the union of the American colonies. It called for the governors to meet and arrange together for the defense of the colonies. Whatever it cost to build forts and raise an army would be paid by the British treasury. The English plan called for the treasury to be repaid by a tax laid on the colonies by an act of Parliament.

The cartoon drawn by Franklin, thought to be America's first political cartoon

Governor William Shirley, c. 1910

Benjamin Franklin was against the English plan. "Compelling the colonies to pay money without their consent," he wrote at the time to Governor Shirley, "would be treating them as a conquered people, and not as true British subjects." Some years later, the same thought would become a battle cry of the Revolution: "Taxation without representation is tyranny!"

In February 1755 two regiments of British soldiers, led by General Edward Braddock, arrived in the colonies to fight the French.

Benjamin Franklin went with his son William to meet Braddock. "I staid with him several Days, Din'd with him daily," Franklin wrote in his autobiography. "I found the General and Officers of the Army extreamly exasperated, on Account of their not being supply'd with Horses and Carriages."

Benjamin Franklin helped out. He wrote a letter to the local newspaper, "To the Inhabitants of the Counties of Lancaster, York & Cumberland," and asked to hire "the best Carriages and Horses." Within two weeks he had one hundred and fifty wagons, six hundred horses to pull the wagons, and two hundred and fifty-nine pack horses for Braddock's army.

Braddock boasted to Benjamin Franklin of his battle plans. He would first take Fort Duquesne from the French, then Fort Niagara and Fort Frontenac. He said, "I see nothing that can obstruct my march."

Franklin warned Braddock that his soldiers must be prepared for surprise attacks, that his long line of marching soldiers "could be cut like a Thread into several Pieces." Benjamin Franklin wrote, "He smil'd at my Ignorance." Soon after that, Braddock and his army started their march north. On July 9, eight miles from Fort Duquesne, they were ambushed. About one thousand were killed, including General Braddock.

French troops and their Native American allies raided farms in the Virginia and Pennsylvania frontier. Entire families on isolated farms were killed, scalped, and left to rot. By fall 1755 frontier settlers were in a panic. They rushed to the nearest cities and towns, including

General Braddock retreating from battle, from an engraving c. 1900

Franklin's Philadelphia. There was a rush to arms, to protect the colony, and a call for Benjamin Franklin to lead the troops.

"I undertook this military Business," Franklin later wrote, "tho' I did not conceive myself well-qualified for it." His more than five hundred volunteer soldiers called him General Franklin. They marched northward, built stockades, and rebuilt forts.

Benjamin Franklin was a resourceful general. The minister who traveled with Franklin's army complained that the men did not come for religious services. "It is perhaps below the Dignity of your Profession," Franklin told the minister, "to act as Steward of the Rum. But if you were to deal it out, and only just after Prayers, you would have them all about you." That's just what the minister did, and Benjamin Franklin reported, "Never were Prayers more generally & more punctually attended."

After just two months as a soldier, General Benjamin Franklin returned to Philadelphia and a hero's welcome. A parade followed him home. Then, at his front door, some soldiers fired off guns in his honor. The gunshots shook a table in his study and broke several glass pieces he used for his electrical experiments.

Despite the honors, Benjamin Franklin wrote, "I had not so good an Opinion of my military Abilities." When the governor asked him to lead an army in battle against a French-held fort, Franklin declined.

Benjamin Franklin was about to serve the colony in a different way.

Small-property owners in Pennsylvania paid taxes to provide for the soldiers' pay and provisions and other colony expenses. But Pennsylvania's biggest landowner, the family of William Penn, paid no taxes. Members of the Assembly needed someone to go to London to talk to the Penn family and, if necessary, even to the king. For this, they chose their leading citizen. They chose Franklin.

10.

FROM THE OLD WORLD
TO THE NEW

On April 4, 1757, Benjamin Franklin began his long journey to London.

Deborah Franklin didn't accompany her husband to England, and she wouldn't let their fourteen-year-old daughter Sally go, either. Perhaps they stayed home because ships then were so small that privacy on board was near impossible, and there was also the danger of bad weather and pirate attacks. At the time, most women didn't make long sea voyages. Or perhaps Deborah stayed home and kept Sally with her simply because she was a homebody. She spent just about her entire life in or around Market Street.

In December 1757 a friend of Franklin's tried to lure Deborah to England. He wrote that the ladies of London found Franklin "perfectly agreeable," and "upon my word I think you should come over, with all convenient speed to look after your interest." But still, Deborah Franklin stayed in Philadelphia.

Benjamin Franklin left Philadelphia with his son William and two servants. They arrived in New York a few days later, the very day their ship was scheduled to leave. But it was no easy matter to cross the

Atlantic while France and England were at war. They waited eleven weeks for permission to sail and Franklin was miserable. He was restless. Idleness just didn't suit the ever busy Benjamin Franklin.

Once at sea, the captain found the ship was sluggish. He had the water casks moved to the front of the ship, and it sailed faster. That made the ever curious Benjamin Franklin wonder about ship design, what would be the best shape for the hull, the best place to put the masts, and where to store the freight. At night, close to the shore of England, the ship almost crashed into some rocks. It was saved by the big, bright light from a lighthouse, and good citizen Franklin resolved to have lighthouses built off America's shore.

The ship landed at Falmouth harbor. Benjamin and William Franklin and their servants then traveled by carriage along the southern coast of England during perhaps its most glorious season, the early days of summer. They made a few sightseeing stops along the way, including one at Stonehenge, and marveled at the mysterious circle of huge

Franklin's maritime ideas, sent in a letter to Alphonsus Le Roy, a friend in Paris

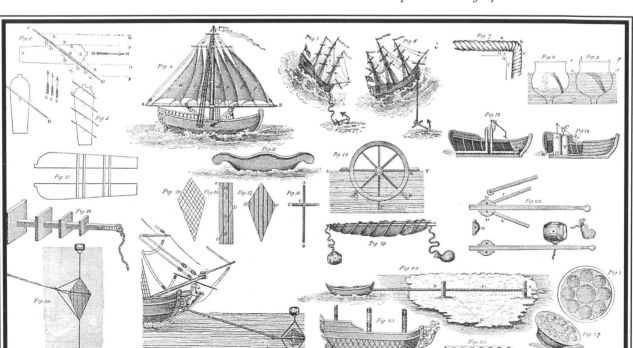

stones made a few thousand years before Benjamin Franklin's time.

Late in the evening of July 26 they arrived at the Bear Inn, near old London Bridge. There they had dinner and took rooms for the night.

Franklin had last been in London in 1726. It was a bigger city now, noisier and busier, with lots more industry. The air was filled with ashes and smoke. The streets were crowded with horse-drawn carriages, well-dressed ladies and gentlemen, beggars, and peddlers.

Benjamin Franklin had been a lowly printer in 1726, with great dreams of success. In 1757 he returned a rich and famous man. Admirers came to call on him. He also went to the very press he had worked at when he was last in London and said to the men there, "Come, my friends, we will drink together." Then this one-time "Water-American" sent for some beer and when it came raised his glass and made the toast, "Success to Printing."

Soon Benjamin Franklin moved into four rooms in the home of Mrs. Margaret Stevenson on Craven Street. He lived there in high style and called Mrs. Stevenson "the good lady of the house." He later wrote that in all the years he lived with her "we never had among us the smallest misunderstanding; our friendship has been all clear sunshine, without the least cloud in its hemisphere."

Mrs. Stevenson took care of Benjamin Franklin, nursed him when he was sick, entertained his friends, and helped choose gifts to send to Mrs. Franklin and Sally. She even tolerated his strange habits, including his morning "air baths."

Deborah Franklin wrote to Benjamin often and he wrote back, but not as often. "At this time of life," Franklin wrote in one of his letters home, "my uneasiness at being absent from my family, and longing desire to be with them, make me often sigh in the midst of cheerful company."

Deborah sent him dried peaches, cranberries, nuts, apples, buckwheat flour, and cornmeal. Benjamin sent her a device to core apples, cloth for curtains, blankets, cloth place mats, and china. He also sent some blue cotton dress goods. "I bought it by candlelight," he wrote, "and liked it then, but not so well afterwards. If you do not fancy it, send it as a present from me to sister Jenny." And he bought two large-print prayer books, for Deborah and the family nurse, Goody Smith, "So you will both of you be reprieved from the use of spectacles in church a little longer."

He also sent home a large jug for beer. "I fell in love with it at first sight," Benjamin wrote Deborah, "for I thought it looked like a fat jolly dame, clean and tidy, with a neat blue and white calico gown on, good natured and lovely, and put me in mind of—somebody."

Benjamin and William Franklin went traveling to Scotland, Belgium, and Holland, where, in Leyden, they visited with Pieter van Musschenbroek, discoverer of the Leyden jar. They traveled also to their ancestral home in Ecton. The relatives they met there were mostly old and poor. The thirty-acre farm and blacksmith shop had been sold to strangers. The old stone cottage was called "the Franklin House," but it was a school now.

Benjamin Franklin met often with Thomas and Richard Penn, sons of William Penn, the founder of Pennsylvania. The Penn brothers were not willing to pay taxes on their American land. At one meeting, Franklin reminded Thomas Penn of his father's promise, that the Pennsylvania Assembly had the power to make laws for Pennsylvania, and Thomas Penn laughed.

William Penn at age 52, from a painting by Francis Place, c. 1690

Thomas Penn, from an engraving by David Martin, c. 1760

King George III, from a painting by Allan Ramsay, c. 1760

Benjamin Franklin spoke with advisors close to King George II. He hired lawyers who negotiated with the Penn brothers' lawyers, and by 1760 they reached a compromise. Some of the Penns' land, the surveyed land, could be taxed. At first, this wasn't a lot of money for the colony, just 2 percent of the total amount raised by taxes. Still, it was a great victory. Benjamin Franklin had won the right to tax the Penns.

Benjamin Franklin was still in London in 1761, the time of the coronation of King George III. He predicted the new king's reign "will be happy and truly glorious," a prediction that Franklin himself would help keep from coming true.

In 1760 Benjamin Franklin became a grandfather by his son, William. At the time, the rumor was that the mother of the boy was some "low woman, a London 'oyster woman.'" The boy was named William Temple Franklin. And just as Benjamin Franklin had married the daughter of his landlady, he wanted his son to marry Mary "Polly" Stevenson, the daughter of their London landlady. But William had other ideas. On September 2, 1762, just three weeks after his father left England, William married Elizabeth Downes, the daughter of a wealthy man who owned a sugar plantation in Barbados.

That day, the *London Chronicle* announced his marriage, and with it, another bit of news about William. "This morning," the *Chronicle* reported, "was married at St. George's Church, Hanover Square, William Franklin Esq., the new appointed Governor of New Jersey, to Miss Elizabeth Downes, on St. James Street."

That was the first public notice of his appointment, the first governor named by King George III. John Penn, Richard Penn's son who was soon to be named governor of Pennsylvania, called this bit of patronage a "shameful affair . . . a dishonor and a disgrace." John Adams attributed the appointment to "backstairs intrigues."

Whatever Benjamin Franklin's part might have been in getting his son the position, he would one day regret it. During the Revolution, William Franklin remained loyal to George III. "Nothing had ever affected him with such keen sensations," a friend wrote of Benjamin Franklin's relations with William, "as to find himself deserted in his old age by his only son."

In August 1762 Benjamin Franklin left England. He was going home.

"I am going to a country and a people that I love," he wrote at the time. "I am going from the old world to the new; and I fancy I feel like those who are leaving this world for the next: grief at the parting; fear for the passage; hope for the future."

11.

THE PAXTON BOYS

On November 1, 1762, Benjamin Franklin returned to Philadelphia. He was happy to be home and the people of Philadelphia were happy to have him. He wrote to a friend that he found "my wife and daughter well; the latter grown quite a woman." She was nineteen now. He wrote that his Philadelphia friends were "as hearty and affectionate as ever."

Franklin was still postmaster of the colonies. In the spring of 1763, he went with his daughter, Sally, on a tour of colonial post offices. When he returned home in November, there was real trouble in Philadelphia.

The French and Indian War had ended in February 1763 with the Treaty of Paris. But there was no peace in the colonies. Native American tribes had fought for both the French and English. Some were still at war. They burned villages in western Pennsylvania and killed settlers. Hundreds of farms were abandoned by frightened colonists.

A gang was formed to avenge the white people who had been killed. They were from the Donegal and Paxton townships. They called themselves "the Paxton Boys."

"On *Wednesday*, the 14th of *December*, 1763, Fifty-seven Men,"

Franklin wrote in a pamphlet, "surrounded the small Village of *Indian* Huts, and just at the Break of Day broke into them all at once. Only three Men, two Women, and a young Boy, were found at Home, the rest being out among the neighboring White People, some to sell the Baskets, Brooms and Bowls they manufactured, and others on other Occasions. These poor defenceless Creatures were immediately fired upon, stabbed and hatcheted to Death! . . . All of them were scalped, and otherwise horribly mangled. Then their Huts were set on Fire, and most of them burnt down."

The Paxton Boys had killed six Conestogas, members of a peace-loving tribe whose ancestors had welcomed the first English to Pennsylvania with food and gifts, and had signed a treaty of friendship with William Penn to last "as long as the sun should shine, or the waters run in the rivers."

Two weeks later, the Paxton Boys returned for the Conestogas not at home that grisly morning of the fourteenth.

"Fifty of them," Benjamin Franklin reported, "armed as before, dismounting, went directly to the Work-house, and by Violence broke open

The Paxton Boys killing Native Americans, from a drawing, c. 1914

the Door, and entered with the utmost Fury in their Countenances.—When the poor Wretches saw they had *no Protection* nigh, nor could possibly escape, and being without the least Weapon for Defence, they divided into their little Families, the Children clinging to their Parents; they fell on their Knees, protested their Innocence, declared their Love to the *English*, and that, in their whole Lives, they had never done them Injury; and in this Posture they all received the Hatchet!—Men, Women and little Children—were every one inhumanly murdered!—in cold Blood!"

Franklin ended his pamphlet, "*Cowards* can handle Arms, can strike where they are sure to meet with no Return, can wound, mangle and murder; but it belongs to *brave* Men to spare, and to protect; for, as the poet says,—*Mercy still sways the Brave.*"

The Paxton Boys were not finished. Several hundred of them, armed with rifles and hatchets, headed east. They were set to kill the more than one hundred peace-loving Native Americans who had run to Philadelphia for protection.

Benjamin Franklin formed an association of some one thousand armed volunteers. Then he and three others rode out to meet the Paxton Boys. He convinced them it was useless to attack. The Paxton Boys rode west again, toward the Pennsylvania frontier.

Benjamin Franklin had rescued Philadelphia and Native Americans from violence, but he had, in his words, "made myself many enemies among the populace." In the 1760s not

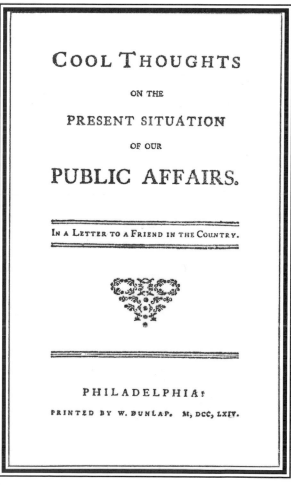

COOL THOUGHTS

ON THE

PRESENT SITUATION

OF OUR

PUBLIC AFFAIRS.

IN A LETTER TO A FRIEND IN THE COUNTRY.

PHILADELPHIA:
PRINTED BY W. DUNLAP. M, DCC, LXIV.

Cover of a 1764 pamphlet written by Franklin calling for a change in the government of Pennsylvania

by the Honourable
John Penn, Esq.

Lieutenant Governor and Commander in Chief, the Province of Pennsylvania, and Counties of New Castle, Kent and Sussex, upon Delaware.

A Proclamation

WHEREAS I have received Information That on *Wednesday*, the Fourteenth Day of this Month, a Number of People, armed, and mounted on Horseback, unlawfully assembled together, and went to the *Indian* Town of the *Constogue* Manor, in *Lancaster* County, and without the Least Reason or Provocation, in cool Blood, barbarously killed six of the *Indians* settled there, and burnt and destroyed all their Houses and Effects: **AND WHEREAS** so cruel and inhuman an Act, committed in the Heart of this Province on the said *Indians*, who have lived peaceably and inoffensively among us, during all our late Troubles, and for many Years before, and were justly considered as under the Protection of this Government and its Laws, calls loudly for the vigorous Exertion of the civil Authority, to detect the Offenders, and bring them to condign Punishment; **I HAVE THEREFORE,** by and with the Advice and Consent of the Council, thought fit to issue this Proclamation, and do hereby strictly charge and enjoin all Judges, Justices, Sheriffs, Constables, Officers Civil and Military, and all other His Majesty's liege subjects within this Province, to make diligent Search and Enquiry after the Authors and Perpetrators of the said Crime, their Abettors and Accomplices, and to use all possible means to apprehend and secure them in some of the public Goals of this Province, that they may be brought to their Trials, and be proceeded against according to Law. **AND WHEREAS** a Number of other *Indians*, who lately lived on or near the Frontiers of this Province, being willing and desirous to preserve and continue to ancient Friendship which heretofore subsisted between them and the good People of this Province, have, at their own earnest Request, been removed from their Habitations, and brought into the County of *Philadelphia* and seated for the present, for their Security, on the *Provinceland*, and in other Places in the Neighborhood of the city of *Philadelphia*, where Provision is made for them at the public Expence; I do therefore hereby strictly forbid all Persons whatsoever, to molest or injure any of the said *Indians*, as they will answer the contrary at their Peril.

GIVEN under my Hand...

John Penn ... GOD save the KING

—Pa Gazette–December 29, 1763

By the Honourable
John Penn, Esq.

Lieutenant Governor and Commander in Chief, the Province of Pennsylvania, and Counties of New Castle, Kent and Sussex, upon Delaware.

A Proclamation

WHEREAS the Delaware and Shawenese Tribes of Indians, and others in Confederacy with them, have, without the least Provocation, and contrary to their late most solemn Treaties, ungratefully renewed War upon this Province, and, in a most cruel, savage and perfidious Manner, killed and butchered great Numbers of the Inhabitants, burnt and destroyed their Habitations, and laid waste the County: **I HAVE THERE-FORE** thought fit, by and with the Advice of the Council, to issue this Proclamation, and do hereby declare the said Delaware and Shawenese Indians and all others, who, in Conjunction with them, have committed hostilities against His Majesty's Subjects within this Province, to be **ENEMIES, REBELS** and **TRAITORS** to His Most Sacred MAJESTY AND I do hereby require all His Majesty's subjects of this Province and earnestly invite those of the neighboring Provinces, to embrace all Opportunities of pursuing, taking, killing, and destroying the said Delaware and Shawenese Indians, and all others concerned in committing Hostilities, Incursions, Murders or Ravages upon this Province ...

I DO HEREBY DECLARE AND PROMISE, That there shall be paid, out of the Monies granted for His Majesty's Use, to all and every Person and Persons not in the pay of this Province, the following several and respective **Premiums** and **Bounties** for the **Prisoners** and **Scalps** of the Enemy Indians that shall be taken or killed within the Bounds of this Province, as limited by the Royal Charter, or in Pursuit from within the said Bounds; that is to say, For every **Male Indian Enemy,** above Ten Years old, who shall be taken Prisoner, and delivered at any Forts garrisoned by the troops in the pay of this Province, or at any of the County Towns, to the Keeper of the common Goals there, the Sum of **ONE HUNDRED AND FIFTY SPANISH DOLLARS,** or **PIECES OF EIGHT,** for every **FEMALE INDIAN ENEMY,** taken Prisoner and brought in as aforesaid; and for every **MALE INDIAN ENEMY,** of Ten Years old or under, taken prisoner and delivered as aforesaid, the Sum of **ONE HUNDRED AND THIRTY PIECES OF EIGHT.** For the Scalp of every **MALE INDIAN ENEMY,** above the Age of Ten Years, produced as Evidence of their being killed, the Sum of **ONE HUNDRED AND THIRTY-FOUR PIECES OF EIGHT.** And for the Scalp of every **FEMALE INDIAN ENEMY,** above the Age of Ten Years, produced as Evidence of their being killed, the Sum of **FIFTY PIECES OF EIGHT.** AND that there shall be paid to every Officer or Officers, Soldier or Soldiers, as are or shall be in the Pay of this Province, who shall take, bring in, and produce any **Indian Enemy Prisoner** or **Scalp** as aforesaid, **ONE HALF** of the said several and respective Premiums and Bounties.

GIVEN under my Hand...

—Pa. Gazette—July 12, 1764.

everyone celebrated saving the lives of Native Americans, even peace-loving ones.

Pamphlets that made heroes of the murderous Paxton Boys were sold in the streets. Governor John Penn blocked any effort to prosecute the Paxton Boys. Instead, he encouraged his citizens to do more killing by setting a reward, a bounty, for anyone bringing in the scalp of a Native American, male or female.

Pennsylvania was a proprietary colony ruled by John Penn. Benjamin Franklin wanted Penn removed from office. Franklin, still a member of the Pennsylvania Assembly, led a crusade to change the government and have Pennsylvania be given a royal charter like eight of the other colonies, and be under the direct control of the king.

There would be an election soon, and the campaign was bitter. Governor Penn called Franklin a black-hearted villain. The governor's supporters called Franklin a man of low morals who had fathered an illegitimate son, accepted bribes, and taken credit for the scientific discoveries of others.

The polls opened at about nine in the morning on October 1, 1764, and remained open through the night, until three o'clock the following afternoon. Old and lame people were carried to the polls on chairs and stretchers.

Benjamin Franklin lost the election by just twenty-five of the four thousand who voted. But his party, made up of people who agreed with him and wanted a change in the government, won a majority of seats in the Assembly.

Soon after the election, the new Assembly met. They voted to send a representative to England, to petition the king to make Pennsylvania a royal colony. They voted again to send Benjamin Franklin.

12.

THE MOTHER OF
MISCHIEFS

One-shilling tax stamp made in 1765 for the American colonies, from a drawing, c. 1850. The stamp was made on dark blue paper with a thin strip of tin foil attached.

On December 10, 1764, Benjamin Franklin arrived in London. The Stamp Act, a tax on newspapers, magazines, almanacs, contracts, marriage licenses, playing cards, and other printed items, was then being debated in Parliament. People in the American colonies would have to buy a stamp and place it on these things to show they paid the tax. The money was needed to help pay the huge cost of the French and Indian War that had just ended. Franklin called the tax "the mother of mischiefs."

This wouldn't be the first tax the colonies would pay their mother country. There had been extra charges, called tariffs, on goods brought into the colonies, and on things made in the colonies and sold elsewhere. In 1764 Parliament passed the Sugar Act, a tax on sugar, molasses, coffee, wine, silk, and certain other imported things. But those tariffs were seen as indirect taxes, a way to regulate trade. Those taxes were paid by ships' captains and merchants, and only indirectly, in the form of higher prices, by colonists. But with the Stamp Act, colonists would directly pay the tax when they bought the stamps.

In February 1765 Benjamin Franklin and three other American agents met with George Grenville, the British prime minister. They argued against the tax, but Grenville was not moved. "You cannot hope to get any good," he said, "by a controversy with the mother country."

"I took every step in my power to prevent the passing of the Stamp Act," Benjamin Franklin wrote in a letter, "but the tide was too strong against us."

The Stamp Act was signed on March 22, 1765, by King George III, to take effect on the first of November 1765.

The stamps were made in England and sent to agents in the colonies who were to sell them. Benjamin Franklin didn't think there would be much protest against the tax. He even suggested that two of his friends, John Hughes of Pennsylvania and Jared Ingersoll of Connecticut, become agents. But in America there was a strong, angry reaction to the stamps. Because Franklin had recommended his friends become agents, he was seen as a traitor.

King George III around 1765, from an engraving by Lossing and Barritt, c. 1850, possibly based on a painting by Sir William Beechey, c. 1797

A mob threatened the Franklins' and Hughes's houses. Deborah Franklin wrote that people had urged her to leave Philadelphia. On September 12 Hughes wrote to Franklin, "I am told my house shall be pull'd down and the stamps burnt."

Deborah Franklin and John Hughes got guns and, with some friends, stood by their homes. Several hundred others gathered to keep the peace and the threat passed. On September 17, Hughes wrote, "We are all yet in the land of the living, and our property safe. Thank God."

In New York, when the stamp agent tried to do his job, a mob stormed his house and destroyed his furniture. In Connecticut Jared Ingersoll's home was attacked. Only in Georgia was the agent able to sell any stamps.

In May 1765 Virginia's House of Burgesses passed a resolution against the Stamp Act. In October representatives from nine colonies met in New York City, protested the tax, and resolved not to buy anything that required a stamp. On November 1, the day the tax took effect, shops were closed and bells tolled to mark the death of American liberty. On some newspapers, where the tax stamp belonged, a skull was printed instead. It soon became clear in England that American colonists refused to pay the tax.

When Benjamin Franklin learned how strong the feelings in America were against the tax, he went to work. "I was extremely busy," he wrote to a friend, "informing, explaining, consulting, disputing, in a continual hurry from morning till night."

There were hearings in Parliament on the tax, and on February 13, 1766, Benjamin Franklin was called before the committee. He answered questions and told of the American people's past love for Great Britain, but said that they would *never* pay the Stamp Act taxes, "unless compelled by force of arms." When American newspapers reported what Benjamin Franklin said, he was no longer considered a traitor to the American cause.

The next week, on February 21, 1766, by a majority of 108 votes, Parliament voted to repeal the Stamp Act.

"My dear Child," Benjamin Franklin wrote to his wife soon after that, "as the Stamp Act is at length repeal'd, I am willing you should have a new Gown, which you may suppose I did not send sooner, as I knew you would not like to be finer than your Neighbors, unless in a Gown of your own Spinning. . . . I send you also a box with three fine Cheeses. Perhaps a Bit of them may be left when I come home. . . . I am very well, and hope this will find you and Sally so with all our Relations and Friends, to whom, my Love, I am, as ever, Your affectionate Husband."

Benjamin Franklin thought his work in England was done. He asked the Pennsylvania Assembly permission to return home. But the Assembly thought differently. Its answer was to reelect him to serve another year as their agent in London. Other colonies made him their agent, too: Georgia in 1768, New Jersey in 1769, and Massachusetts in 1770.

The Boston Massacre, from an engraving, c. 1900

Even with the repeal of the Stamp Act, conflicts between England and the American colonies did not end. There were new taxes, town meetings, protests, and a boycott of British goods. On March 5, 1770, in Boston, a group of British soldiers fired at a threatening mob of patriots. Five Americans were killed and six injured in what was later called the Boston Massacre.

One day in November 1772, Franklin complained to a member of Parliament about British goings-on in the colonies, especially the keeping of troops in Boston. Franklin was told Americans wanted these measures taken. Franklin couldn't believe such a thing. He was outraged. A few days later, the Englishman proved it. He showed Franklin a packet of letters written by Thomas Hutchinson, the royal governor of Massachusetts, and by Andrew Oliver, the lieutenant governor, that called for a strong British hand in dealing with American patriots. Franklin sent the letters to Thomas Cushing, Speaker of the Massachu-

Sam Adams, from an engraving by
Lossing and Barritt, c. 1850

setts House of Representatives, with instructions on who should see the letters and that they must not be reprinted.

"Three may keep a secret," Benjamin Franklin wrote in his 1735 almanac, "if two of them are dead." The secret of the Hutchinson letters, as they were called, was soon no secret at all.

The letters were passed around among members of the Committee of Correspondence, and then to others. Sam Adams read them to the House. John Adams showed them everywhere, even to his aunt. Reprinted copies of the letters reached each of the thirteen colonies, and England.

The letters caused an uproar on both sides of the Atlantic.

In Massachusetts the House called for the removal of Hutchinson and Oliver from office. In August 1773 Benjamin Franklin forwarded the request to an agent of the king.

In London it was suspected that John Temple had sent the letters to America. He declared he hadn't and dueled Thomas Whately over the matter.

First Temple and Whately fired pistols at each other. They both missed. Then they dueled with swords. Temple was a skilled swordsman, but deaf. He stuck his sword in Whately's side. Whately was bloodied and had had enough. He called for an end to the fight, but Temple didn't hear him. Temple struck again. Whately fell. Temple was deaf, but he wasn't blind. He saw Whately on the ground and stopped the fight.

When Benjamin Franklin learned of the fight, he wrote to a London newspaper, "Sir, Finding that two gentlemen have been unfortunately engaged in a duel about a transaction and its circumstances of which both of them are totally ignorant and innocent, I think it incumbent upon me to declare (for the prevention of further mischief, as far as such a declaration may contribute to prevent it) that I alone am the person who obtained and transmitted to Boston the letters in question." But

Benjamin Franklin never told who gave him the letters, just that he was a "gentleman of character and distinction."

In America tempers were rising. At about this time, patriots dumped 342 chests of tea into Boston harbor.

Benjamin Franklin didn't approve. He called the action a "violent injustice." But news of the Boston Tea Party didn't distract Franklin's enemies.

Soon after his letter appeared in the London newspaper, Benjamin Franklin was called before a committee of Parliament. Franklin explained that the Hutchinson letters were about public matters, so they were not private.

The British people did not accept his explanation. Samuel Johnson, a great English writer, called Franklin "the master of mischief."

"He has forfeited all the respect of societies and of men," Alexander Wedderburn, the king's representative, said of Franklin. "He will henceforth esteem it a libel to be called 'a man of letters.'"

Shortly after his appearance at Parliament, Benjamin Franklin was dismissed by the king's representatives from his office of Deputy Postmaster of America.

Tempers were rising in England too. Early in 1774 Parliament passed a series of laws that, among other things, closed the port of Boston and forced American colonists to feed and house British soldiers. American colonists called these laws the Intolerable Acts.

Later in 1774, in the summer, Franklin met Thomas Paine, a former sailor, corset maker, and tobacco shop owner who would help push American colonists to revolution.

"Mr. Thomas Paine," Franklin wrote to his son-in-law, "is very well recommended to me, as an ingenious, worthy young man. He goes to Pennsylvania with a view of settling there. I request you give him your best advice and countenance, as he is quite a stranger there."

Thomas Paine, from a drawing by Benson J. Lossing, c. 1850, copied from a wax medallion made in 1798, when Paine was in Paris

Franklin's son-in-law helped Paine get settled. Soon after that, Thomas Paine wrote his pamphlet *Common Sense*. It convinced many Americans they must break away from England.

On September 5, 1774, the Continental Congress met in Philadelphia. The delegates declared that Parliament and the king had no right to rule the colonies. But they weren't ready for revolution. They petitioned King George III. They called him a "loving father" and hoped that his "royal authority and interposition may be used for our relief." They sent the petition to Benjamin Franklin.

Franklin brought the petition to King George III, who sent it to Parliament. The members of Parliament were in no mood to compromise. In a bitter debate, they characterized American colonists as cowards who would run from the mere sound of cannon fire.

At about the time Benjamin Franklin was busy with the petition, his wife Deborah was sick and dying. In December 1774 she was felled by a stroke. Five days later, she died, reportedly "without a struggle or a groan."

Thirty years earlier, Benjamin Franklin wrote this song, "My Plain Country Joan," in praise of his wife:

Of their Chloes and Phyllises poets may prate,
    I sing my plain country Joan,
These twelve years my wife, still the joy of my life,
    Blest day that I made her my own.
Not a word of her face, of her shape, or her air,
    Or of flames, or of darts, you shall hear;
I beauty admire, but virtue I prize,
    That fades not in seventy year.
Am I loaded with care, she takes off a large share,
    That the burden ne'er makes me to reel;
Does good fortune arrive, the joy of my wife
    Quite doubles the pleasure I feel.

She defends my good name, even when I'm to blame,
    Firm friend as to man e'er was given;
Her compassionate breast feels for all the distressed,
    Which draws down more blessings from heaven.

During the ten years Franklin was in London, he and Deborah continually sent each other letters and gifts. Benjamin sent her elegant clothes, but Deborah refused to wear them. She wouldn't dress up while her husband was away. Each spring, Franklin planned to return home by fall and each fall he stayed on. When he left Philadelphia in 1764, he expected to be apart from Deborah for just a short while, but with her death, the parting was forever.

13.

THE BROKEN VASE

America was headed toward revolution and Benjamin Franklin was headed home.

"The unity of the British empire in all its parts was a favorite idea of his," Dr. Joseph Priestley, the English clergyman, chemist, and discoverer of oxygen, said of his friend Benjamin Franklin. "He used to compare it to a beautiful china vase, which, if ever broken, could never be put together again."

Franklin spent his last day in London with Priestley. "I think I knew him as well as one man can generally know another," Priestley said later. He said Franklin didn't want a break with Britain, but hoped the mother country's differences with its colonies could be addressed.

Together they read the latest American newspapers to reach them. They learned of the unrest in America and talked of the prospects of war. "He was frequently not able to proceed," Priestley said later, "for the tears literally running down his cheeks."

On March 21, 1775, Benjamin Franklin left England.

On April 19, while Franklin was at sea, in Lexington, Massachusetts, a British Royal Marine major and his troops came upon some seventy armed American patriot soldiers. "Disperse ye Rebels!" the major called. As the Americans began to scatter, one of them fired a shot, the "shot heard round the world." The British fired back and there was war, the American Revolution.

The china vase was broken.

On May 5, 1775, Benjamin Franklin arrived in Philadelphia. On May 6 he was elected by the Pennsylvania Assembly as their delegate to the Second Continental Congress.

The people of Philadelphia were busy preparing for war. Patriots fortified the port and searched the mail for treasonous letters. If they found anyone disloyal to the cause of the Revolution, they forced him to stand on a cart, admit his errors, and ask the crowd gathered to forgive him. If he refused to ask for forgiveness, he was tarred and feathered.

"You are as a Member of Parliament, and one of that Majority

The Battle of Lexington, from an engraving by Benson J. Lossing, c. 1900

which has doomed my Country to Destruction," Benjamin Franklin wrote to his friend William Strahan on July 5, 1775, in a letter he never sent. "You have begun to burn our Towns, and murder our People—Look upon your Hands!—They are stained with the Blood of your Relations!—You and I were long Friends:—You are now my Enemy."

Benjamin Franklin could have written a similar letter to his son, William.

Soon after his return to America, Franklin visited with his son in Perth Amboy, then the capital of New Jersey. Benjamin Franklin was a staunch patriot, convinced by then of the need to fight the British. William, still the royal governor of New Jersey, remained loyal to the king. Each Franklin tried to convince the other to change his view, and neither succeeded.

Franklin's letter to Strahan

Philadelphia

AFFIDAVITS and depositions relative to the commencement of the late hostilities in the province of Massachusetts Bay . . .
Charles **Thomson**, Secretary

Lexington, April 25, 1775

We Solomon Brown, Jonathan Loring, and Elijah Sanderson; all of lawful age, and of Lexington, in the county of Middlesex, and colony of Massachusetts-Bay in New England, do testify and declare that on the evening of the 18th of April instant, being on the road between Concord and Lexington, and all of us mounted on horses, we were about ten of the clock, suddenly surprised by nine persons, whom we took to be regular officers, who rode up to us mounted and armed, each having a pistol in his hand, and after putting pistols to our breasts, and seizing the bridles of our horses, they swore that if we stirred another step, we should all be dead men, upon which we surrendered ourselves; they detained us until two o'clock the next morning, in which time they searched and greatly abused us, having first enquired about the Magazine at Concord, whether any guards were posted there, and whether the bridges were up, and said four or five regiments of Regulars would be in possession of the stores soon—they then brought us back to Lexington, cut the horses bridles and girths, turned them loose and then left us.

Solomon Brown, Jonathan Loring,
Elijah Sanderson.

I Elijah Sanderson, above named, do further testify and declare, that I was on Lexington common the morning of the 19th of April aforesaid, having been dismissed by the officers abovementioned, and saw a large body of regular troops advancing towards Lexington company, many of whom were then dispersing—I heard one of the regulars whom I took to be an officer say, "damn them we will have them," and immediately the regulars shouted aloud, ran and fired on the Lexington company, which did not fire a gun before the regulars discharged on them. Eight of the Lexington company were killed, while they were dispersing, and at a considerable distance from each other, and many wounded, and although a spectator, I narrowly escaped with my life.

Elijah Sanderson.

I John Robins, being of lawful age, do testify and say, that on the nineteenth instant, the company under the command of Capt. John Parker being drawn up (sometime before sunrise) on the green or common, and I being in the front rank, there suddenly appeared a number of the King's troops, about a thousand, as I thought, at the distance of about 60 or 70 yards from us, buzzing, and on a quick pace toward us, with three officers in their front on horseback, and on full gallop towards us, the foremost of which cried, "throw down your arms, ye villains, ye rebels," upon which said company dispersing, the foremost of the three officers ordered their men, saying, "Fire, by God fire," at which moment we received a heavy and close fire from them, at which instant being wounded, I fell, and several of our men were shot dead by me: Captain Parker's men, I believe, had not then fired a gun: And further the deponent saith not.

John Robins.

I John Parker, of lawful age, and commander of the militia in Lexington, do testify and declare, that on the 19th instant, in the morning, about one of the clock, being informed that there were a number of regular officers riding up and down the road, stopping and insulting people as they passed the road; and also was informed, that a number of regular troops were on their march from Boston, in order to take the province stores at Concord; ordered our militia to meet on the common in said Lexington, to consult what to do, and concluded not to be discovered, nor meddle or make with said regular troops (if they should approach) unless they should insult or molest us, and upon their sudden approach I immediately ordered our militia to disperse, and not to fire; immediately said troops made their appearance and rushed furiously, fired upon and killed 8 of our party, without receiving any provocation therefor from us.

John Parker.

George Washington, from an engraving by Benson J. Lossing, c. 1900

Abigail Adams, from an engraving, based on a portrait by Benjamin Blyth, c. 1766

In July 1776 William Franklin was jailed for "perplexing the cause of liberty and in serving the designs of the British king." A newspaper report of the arrest also noted, "He is the son of Dr. Benjamin Franklin, the genius of the day, and the great patron of American liberty."

Early reports of the Revolution were discouraging. In October 1775 the second Continental Congress had bad news from General Washington. His ragtag army was falling apart. He had no winter clothing for his men, poor shelter, not enough food, and almost no gunpowder. His troops were eager to quit. The Congress sent Franklin and two other delegates to Cambridge, Massachusetts. There they met with General Washington and helped him plan for a more disciplined, better supplied army.

While Benjamin Franklin was in Cambridge, he dined with Abigail Adams. "I found him social but not talkative," Mrs. Adams wrote, but "when he spoke, something useful dropped from his tongue." She also felt she could read into Franklin's heart, and there she found "patriotism shone in its full luster."

As Franklin was set to leave for home, word came that a British battleship had bombarded Portland, Maine, a defenseless city. The church, other public buildings, and one hundred and thirty houses were destroyed. British soldiers landed and set fire to buildings and boats.

Benjamin Franklin was horrified.

"Whenever kings," he wrote, "instead of protecting the lives and properties of their subjects, as is their bounded duty, do endeavor to perpetrate the destruction of either, they thereby cease to be kings, become tyrants, and dissolve all ties of allegiance between themselves and their people."

In the end of March 1776, Benjamin Franklin was sent on another mission, this time to Montreal, to enlist French Canada to join the colonies in their revolution. It was a long, difficult journey. By the time he reached Saratoga, Franklin was exhausted. "I have undertaken a fatigue," he wrote, "which, at my time of life, may prove too much for me." He wrote letters of farewell to some of his friends.

Benjamin Franklin survived the journey, but his mission failed.

Soon after his return, Franklin served on a committee of five elected by the Second Continental Congress to draft the Declaration of Independence. But the draft was written by just one member of the committee, Thomas Jefferson of Virginia.

"I wish I had written it myself," Franklin told Jefferson. Then he made a few suggestions, among them that "We hold these truths to be sacred and undeniable!" be changed to "We hold these truths to be self-evident."

On July 2, 1776, members of the Continental Congress voted for independence. Then, for three days, they discussed each line of Jefferson's draft of the Declaration of Independence.

Benjamin Franklin, Thomas Jefferson, John Adams, Robert Livingston, and Roger Sherman discussing the Declaration of Independence, from an engraving, c. 1900

A Declaration by the Representatives of the UNITED STATES OF AMERICA, in General Congress assembled.

When in the course of human events it becomes necessary for one people to dissolve the political bands which have connected them with another, and to ~~advance from that subordination in which they have hitherto remained, & to~~ assume among the powers of the earth the separate and equal ~~equal & independent~~ station to which the laws of nature & of nature's god entitle them, a decent respect to the opinions of mankind requires that they should declare the causes which impel them to the ~~change~~ separation.

We hold these truths to be self-evident; ~~sacred & undeniable~~, that all men are created equal ~~& independent~~, that they are endowed by their creator with ~~equal rights, some~~ ~~from that equal creation they derive~~ inherent & inalienable rights; that among these ~~which~~ are ~~the preservation of life, & liberty, & the pursuit of happiness; that to secure these rights ~~ends~~, governments are instituted among men, deriving their just powers from the consent of the governed; that whenever any form of government ~~shall~~ becomes destructive of these ends, it is the right of the people to alter or to abolish it, & to institute new government, laying it's foundation on such principles & organising it's powers in such form, as to them shall seem most likely to effect their safety & happiness. prudence indeed will dictate that governments long established should not be ~~changed~~ for light & transient causes: and accordingly all experience hath shewn that mankind are more disposed to suffer while evils are sufferable, than to right themselves by abolishing the forms to which they are accustomed. but when a long train of abuses & usurpations [begun at a distinguished period & pursuing invariably the same object, evinces a design to ~~subject~~ reduce them + under absolute Despotism ~~to arbitrary power~~, it is their right, it is their duty, to throw off such ~~government~~ + & to provide new guards for their future security. such has been the patient sufferance of these colonies; & such is now the necessity which constrains them to expunge their former systems of government. the history of ~~his~~ the present King of Great Britain. is a history of [unremitting] injuries and usurpations, [among which appears no solitary fact ~~to contradict the uniform tenor of the rest but all have~~ in direct object the establishment of an absolute tyranny over these states. to prove this, let facts be submitted to a candid world, [for the truth of which we pledge a faith yet unsullied by falsehood]

A rough draft of the Declaration of Independence

Throughout the debate, Thomas Jefferson recalled later, he sat "by Dr. Franklin, who perceived that I was not insensible to these mutilations. 'I have made it a rule,' said he, 'whenever in my power, to avoid becoming the draftsman of papers to be reviewed by a public body.'"

Then Benjamin Franklin took some of the sting out of all the criticism. He lightened Thomas Jefferson's mood with a story of a group of friends who met to discuss a much smaller set of words. He told Jefferson of a friend who decided to put this sign outside his shop: JOHN THOMPSON, HATTER, MAKES AND SELLS HATS FOR READY MONEY, with a picture of a hat beside the sign.

According to Franklin's story, John Thompson showed the proposed sign to his friends and asked for their suggestions. The friends told Thompson that *Hatter* was unnecessary since *makes Hats* was already on the sign. *Makes* was eliminated because no one would care that he made the hats, just that he sold them. *For ready Money* was dropped, because how else would he sell them? *Sells* was dropped because who would expect the hats to be given away free? And at last *Hats* was dropped, because with the picture everyone would know what John Thompson was selling. In the end, Franklin told Jefferson, all that was left was JOHN THOMPSON and the picture of a hat.

John Hancock, from a drawing by Lossing and Barritt. c. 1850

On July 4, 1776, the Declaration of Independence was approved by Congress. On July 8, it was read to the public outside the Philadelphia State House. The signing didn't begin until August. John Hancock, president of the Congress, was the first to sign and wrote his name in large, bold letters, an extra act of defiance. Benjamin Franklin signed his name with a flourish, a swirl of lines beneath his signature.

In September Benjamin Franklin was sent by Congress to New York to discuss peace with his friend British Admiral Richard Howe. John Adams and Edward Rutledge were sent, too.

Lord Richard Howe, from a drawing by Lossing and Barritt. c. 1850

The roads and inns were crowded. When the men reached New Brunswick, Benjamin Franklin and John Adams shared a small room for the night.

"The window was open, and I," Adams later wrote, "shut it closed. 'Oh!' says Franklin, 'don't shut the window, we shall be suffocated.... Come, open the window and come to bed, and I will convince you.... The Doctor then began a harangue upon air and cold, and respiration, with which I was so much amused that I soon fell asleep, and left him and his philosophy together."

The next day Franklin and Adams met with Howe. "America cannot return to the domination of Great Britain," Benjamin Franklin told the British admiral. And Howe replied, "I have not the authority, nor do I ever expect to have, to treat with the colonies as states independent of the crown of Great Britain."

The mission failed.

By July New York harbor was crowded with British vessels. Admiral Howe had thirteen thousand seamen under his command. His brother, General William Howe, commanded an army of more than thirty thousand well-equipped soldiers. Congress resolved to send Benjamin Franklin to France to seek its help.

"I am old and good for nothing," the seventy-year-old Benjamin Franklin said at the time, "and you may have me for what you please."

The flag of the United States, 1777

14.

HUZZAH! HUZZAH!

Benjamin Franklin sailed to France aboard a small, fast ship, the *Reprisal*. He went with two of his grandsons, seventeen-year-old William Temple Franklin and seven-year-old Benjamin Franklin Bache.

A steady, strong but cold wind sped Franklin and his grandsons across the Atlantic. The strong wind saved them: the *Reprisal* was chased several times by British ships but never caught. Then, near the coast of France, the men of the *Reprisal* captured two British merchant ships.

The trip must have been a great adventure for his grandsons, but Benjamin Franklin was already an old man. He suffered from kidney stones and gout (painful swelling of his joints) and itchy, scaly skin. He was surely glad when on December 3, 1776, the *Reprisal* landed safely on the French coast.

William Temple Franklin, from an etching by Albert Rosenthal, after a painting by John Trumbull, c. 1790

It was still a long way to Paris. Franklin and his grandsons boarded a carriage for the more than three-hundred-mile journey. "The carriage was a miserable one," Franklin wrote in his journal, "with tired horses, the evening dark, scarce a traveler but ourselves on the road; and to make it more *comfortable*, the driver stopped near a wood we were to pass through, to tell us that a gang of eighteen robbers infested that wood, who but two weeks ago had robbed and murdered some travelers on that very spot."

Franklin and his grandsons passed safely through the wood and stopped just outside Nantes, a city near the coast. He hoped to rest there at the country home of a friend, someone he had met in America. But soon, it seemed, all of Nantes was at the house to see the great Franklin. Women saw his fur cap and copied it with a new hairstyle, their hair in curls atop their heads, called *"Coiffure à la Franklin."*

On December 21, Franklin and his grandsons arrived in Paris, a city, in 1776, of more than 500,000 people. It had wide boulevards, narrow, unpaved, muddy side streets, lots of churches, hundreds of hotels, and more than two thousand bakeries. A river, the Seine, runs through its center. During Benjamin Franklin's time, the river was crowded with barges and laundry boats.

Benjamin Franklin arrived in Paris to a great welcome.

"I know all hearts rejoice with me on this occasion," Silas Deane, the American agent already in Paris, wrote to a friend. "Here is the hero, and philosopher, and patriot, all united in this celebrated American."

"That there was scarcely a peasant or a citizen, *a valet de chambre,* coachman or footman, a lady's chambermaid or a scullion in a kitchen," John Adams wrote in his autobiography, "who was not familiar with it [Franklin's name], and who did not consider him as a friend to human kind."

Silas Deane, from a drawing by Lossing and Barritt. c. 1850

Prints, medals, rings, lids of boxes, and watchcases were decorated with his portrait. Statuettes and dolls were made to resemble him. Benjamin Franklin wrote to his daughter in 1779 that it all made "your father's face as well known as that of the moon."

Franklin settled himself first in hotels, then in Passy, a suburb of Paris, in an apartment on the estate of a wealthy businessman. "I live in a fine airy House upon a Hill, which has a large Garden with fine Walks in it, about 1/2 an hours Drive from the City of Paris," he wrote to his sister Jane. "I walk a little every Day in the Garden, have a good Appetite & sleep well . . . upon the whole I live as comfortably as a Man can well do so far from his Home and his Family."

A medallion made of Franklin in 1777, when he was in Passy, from a drawing by Lossing and Barritt, c. 1850

Benjamin Franklin lived *very* comfortably. He had several servants, a well-stocked wine cellar, and horses and a carriage kept ready for him. And he had an important job to do. The Americans didn't think they could win the Revolution without French help. It was Franklin's job to get it.

When he first arrived, there was bad news from America. In August 1776 the British pushed Washington's forces off Long Island and the French were not ready to openly side with the patriots. They didn't want to side with the Americans if it seemed they would lose the war.

A year later, the news was better for the patriots. The British lost the Second Battle of Saratoga; 5,700 British soldiers were captured along with lots of guns and ammunition. The time was right for an agreement with the French. In February 1778 Benjamin Franklin and other agents of America and France signed the Treaty of Alliance, "to maintain effectually the liberty, sovereignty, and independence, absolute and unlimited, of the United States."

When news of the treaty reached America, General Washington had thirteen cannons fired to salute it. His soldiers called out, "Huzzah! Long live the king of France! Huzzah! Long live the friendly European powers! Huzzah for the American states!"

One month later, in March 1778, the American agents, now allies of France, were presented at Versailles to King Louis XVI. This was

Benjamin Franklin's celebrated bareheaded visit to the palace at Versailles.

While he was in France, Benjamin Franklin sent letters of recommendation to General Washington along with two men who greatly helped the Revolution: Baron von Steuben, a Prussian army officer, and the Marquis de Lafayette, a French statesman and soldier. Von Steuben trained and drilled Washington's men until they became a well-disciplined army. Lafayette joined Washington's staff. Both men served in the final great battle of the Revolution, at Yorktown, Virginia.

During his long stay in France, the ever busy, ever social Benjamin Franklin wasn't always at work for the American cause. He dined out almost every night. And he had many flirtations.

"Somebody," Franklin explained in a letter, "gave it out that I lov'd Ladies; and then every body presented me their Ladies (or the Ladies presented themselves) to be *embrac'd*, that is, to have their Necks kiss'd. For as to kissing Lips or Cheeks it is not the Mode here, the first, is reckon'd rude, & the other may rub off the Paint."

While in France, one of Benjamin Franklin's favorite women friends was Madame Helvétius, a witty, wealthy widow. She lived in Paris surrounded by her pets—eighteen cats, ten dogs, and many birds.

"Her hair was frizzled," Abigail Adams wrote of Madame Helvétius. "Over it she had a small straw hat, with a dirty gauze half-handkerchief round it. And a bit of dirtier gauze scarf thrown over her shoulders." Mrs. Adams met her at a dinner party. "After dinner she [Madame Helvétius] threw herself upon a settee, where she showed more than her feet. She had a little lap-dog, who was, next to the Doctore [Franklin] her favorite. This she kissed, and when he wet the floor, she wiped it up with her chemise." Mrs. Adams also wrote, "I own I was highly disgusted, and never wish for an acquaintance with any ladies of this cast."

Franklin proposed marriage to Madame Helvétius. She refused him.

Another favorite of Benjamin Franklin's was the much younger Madame Brillon, whom he called "my daughter." She called him "Papa."

The surrender at Yorktown, from an engraving by Lossing and Barritt, c. 1850

During the summer, Benjamin Franklin visited Madame Brillon usually twice a week. He sat on her terrace, drank tea, and played chess. One evening they played chess while Madame Brillon soaked in a covered bathtub.

Along with his flirtations, chess was another of Benjamin Franklin's favorite pastimes. "One evening," his grandson William later wrote, "he sat at that amusement from six in the afternoon till sunrise." William also wrote of a time his grandfather mixed the game with his politics.

In chess each player has sixteen pieces; the most important among them is the king. If a player's king is taken, his game is lost. "He is a tyrant," Benjamin Franklin once said of his chess king. "I can do without him, and will fight the rest of the battle, *en Republicain* [as a democracy]."

The tyrant king Franklin was really speaking of was King George III of England. And on October 19, 1781, that king lost his hold on his subjects in the thirteen American colonies. In Yorktown, Virginia, about one-fourth of the British soldiers then in America put down their

Lord Charles Cornwallis, from an engraving by Lossing and Barritt, c. 1850, after an English print

weapons, and General Charles Cornwallis surrendered to General George Washington.

"Oh God! It is all over! Oh God! It is all over!" said Lord North, Britain's prime minister, again and again when he heard of it. That surrender ended the last major battle of the Revolutionary War.

Benjamin Franklin, John Adams, and John Jay negotiated peace with Great Britain. On September 3, 1783, they signed the Treaty of Paris. In it, Britain recognized the United States as an independent nation. The treaty set the new country's borders, east to west from the Atlantic Ocean to the Mississippi River, and north to south from Canada to Florida.

With the treaty signed, Benjamin Franklin looked forward to going home. While he waited for the permission of Congress to leave France, he kept busy with visits to his friends and with correspondence.

"My Dear Child," he wrote to his daughter, Sally, in January 1784, "For my own part, I wish the Bald Eagle had not been chosen as the Representative of our Country; he is a Bird of bad moral Character; he does not get his living honestly; you may have seen him perch'd on some dead Tree, near the River where, too lazy to fish for himself, he watches the Labour of the Fishing-Hawk; and, when that diligent Bird has at length taken a Fish, and is bearing it to his Nest for the support of his Mate and young ones, the Bald Eagle pursues him, and takes it from him. . . . The Turk'y is in comparison a much more respectable Bird."

"Dear Sir," he wrote to his English friend William Strahan in February 1784, "I lament with you the political Disorders England at present labours under. . . . In my humble Opinion, the Root of the Evil lies not so much in too long, or too unequally chosen Parliaments, as in the enormous Salaries, Emoluments, and Patronage of your great Offices; and that you will never be at rest till they are all abolish'd, and every place of Honour made at the same time, instead of a Place of Profit, a

July 5. Yesterday, the 4th of July, afforded a spectacle equally awful and grand. The inhabitants of the whole continent of America eagerly devoted in commemorating the anniversary of the greatest revolution that ever took place — — — the expulsion of tyranny and slavery, and the introduction of freedom, happiness and independence, throughout the greatest continent in the world.

At half past nine, the Militia and a detachment of the Continental Artillery with field-pieces and a band of music, colours, &c. paraded in Meeting Street, for the purpose of receiving his Excellency the Governor, who the Privy Council, major General Greene, General Giff, all the civil officers of the State, and a number of officers of the army, assembled at the house of the Hon. William Hazel Gibbes, Esq; from which, about eleven, they preceded in the following order; His Excellency the Governor, preceded by the Sheriff with the Sword of State; the Messenger of the Council bearing a Tipstaff, Major General Greene, General Giff, the Privy Council, and the officers of the State, &c. walked in front of the Artillery and Militia, who received the procession with presented arms; the officers saluting his Excellency as he passed long the line — — — a fende joye was then fired, after which his Excellency, attended by the above, and other gentlemen, retired to his own house, where the company were regaled with a very elegant cold collation.

About three o'clock a most numerous company assembled at the State-house, for the purpose of dining with the Governor, amongst whom were the above gentlemen, many of the members of both Houses, and most of the officers of the Southern army and of the Militia. The dinner, which was elegant and plentiful, and the liquors remarkably good, were served up about four; after which the following toasts were given:

1. The United States of America. — — — Artillery firing 13 rounds, music playing, God save the Thirteen States.

2. May this State be as wise, happy and great, as free, sovereign and independent. Artillery 13, The band playing.

3. The Congress. Artillery 13, the band playing Jove in his Chair.

4. Our generous and illustrious Ally, His Most Christian Majesty. Artillery 13, the band playing, the King of France's guard march.

(It must have afforded uncommon pleasure to the numerous French gentlemen present, several of whom have distinguished themselves in our service, to observe the singularly marking manner in which the name of this illustrious Prince was received — — — No temptations of England, however great, will ever seduce the affection of America from France. Her attachment to that nation will grow, in proportion as leisure permits her to reflect on the glorious, generous, and disinterested part she has acted in forwarding her emancipation.)

5. The United Provinces of Holland. Artillery 13, the band playing.

6. His Excellency General Washington and the Army, thanks to them, and may they be enabled to retire with satisfaction from the field of victory and glory they have gained with a bravery, perseverance, and patriotic virtue, unparalleled in the history extant. Artillery 13, the band playing, The Hero comes.

7. Our ministers abroad. Artillery 13, the band playing.

8. With agriculture, commerce and liberty, may morality, learning and science flourish. Artillery 13, band playing.

9. May we profit by the errors of those nations who have experienced the effects of ambition, vain glory, tyranny, deceit and treachery. Artillery 13, the band playing.

10. May candor, truth, good faith, justice, honor and benevolence, ever be the characteristics of the United States of America. Artillery 13, band playing.

11. May there be no strife among the United States, saving that of excelling each other in a wise policy. Artillery 13, band playing.

12. This glorious day, by which we secured, among the powers of the earth, the separate and equal station, to which the laws of nature and of nature's God entitle us. Artillery 13, band playing.

13. A lasting and happy peace, and to the memory of our patriotic brethren, who greatly fell in obtaining it, by sea or land. Artillery firing 13 minute guns, the band playing a very solemn dirge, for the space of 13 minutes.

... At night a grand display of fireworks was exhibited at the Change, under the direction of Col. Sens, in the front of which were placed several emblematical devices, with pertinent inscriptions; the execution of the whole did honour to the taste of the Colonel, and gave great satisfaction to the spectators.

The city was grandly illuminated, and the day ended with great happiness and pleasure, no accident having happened. It should be mentioned, to the credit of the Fire-masters, that, to prevent any danger from fire, all the engines were ordered out, and placed in different parts of the town.

place of Expence and burthen.... So if you have not Sense and Virtue enough to govern yourselves, e'en dissolve your present old crazy Constitution, and *send members to Congress.* You will say my *Advice* 'smells of *Madeira.*' You are right. This foolish Letter is mere chitchat *between ourselves* over the *second bottle.*"

In May 1784 he wrote to the Reverend Samuel Mather, the son of the Reverend Cotton Mather of Boston: "When I was a boy, I met with a book, entitled *'Essays to do Good'* which I think was written by your father. It had been so little regarded by a former possessor, that several leaves of it were torn out; but the remainder gave me such a turn of thinking, as to have an influence on my conduct through life; for I have always set a great value on the character of a *doer of good,* than on any other kind of reputation; and if I have been, as you seem to think, a useful citizen, the public owes the advantage of it to that book."

This "useful citizen" was soon to be on his way home.

On March 7, 1785, a resolution was passed in Congress permitting "the Honorable Benjamin Franklin, Esquire, to return to America as soon as convenient." Thomas Jefferson was appointed the new ambassador to France.

"You replace Dr. Franklin, I hear," a French minister said to Jefferson. "No one can *replace* him," was Jefferson's reply. He was simply following the great Benjamin Franklin.

Franklin at the signing of the treaty with France, from a painting by Charles E. Mills, c. 1910

15.

A DYING MAN

On July 12, 1785, when Benjamin Franklin left Paris, he carried with him a parting gift from King Louis XVI of France, a portrait of the king with four hundred and eight diamonds arranged in two circles around the picture. The gift was worth, at the time, ten thousand dollars, a great fortune.

On July 22 he boarded a boat that crossed the Channel and brought him to England. There, Benjamin Franklin met his son, William, for the last time. It was not a warm reunion. It was more a business meeting. The elder Franklin signed some papers and gave his son the power to collect some money owed to him. On July 28 Benjamin Franklin left for the United States.

The sea voyage gave Franklin a chance to reflect on his long, productive life and to think about his future. He looked forward to again walking the streets of "dear Philadelphia." He hoped to visit New York and Boston. But the people of Pennsylvania had other plans for their leading citizen.

Soon after Benjamin Franklin reached Philadelphia, he was elected by the Assembly to be president of the Supreme Executive Council of

Franklin returning to Philadelphia, from a drawing by Victor A. Searles, c. 1897

Pennsylvania, a kind of governor. "I find myself harnessed again," Franklin wrote a friend. "They engrossed the prime of my life. They have eaten my flesh, and seem resolved now to pick my bones."

In 1787 Benjamin Franklin was reelected president of Pennsylvania. His election would have been unanimous, except for one vote. The dissenting vote was his own.

Benjamin Franklin was home again in his house on Market Street. He lived there with Sally and some of her seven children. "The companions of my youth," Benjamin Franklin wrote in 1786, at the age of eighty, "are indeed almost all departed, but I find an agreeable society among their children and grandchildren."

While Pennsylvania was prosperous and running well, the new United States was not. It was just a loose union of thirteen states. In 1787 Benjamin Franklin was one of fifty-five delegates from twelve of the states, all but Rhode Island, who met in Philadelphia to remake the government.

It was difficult for eighty-one-year-old Benjamin Franklin to walk the few blocks from his house to the Pennsylvania State House, where the meetings were held, so he was carried there on a chair by inmates of a nearby prison. It was difficult for him to stand for long periods of time, so he often wrote out what he wanted to say and gave it to someone else to read aloud.

The Pennsylvania State House in 1774, from an engraving by Lossing and Barritt, c. 1850

"I am apprehensive," Benjamin Franklin said, "perhaps too apprehensive—that the Government of these States may in future times end in a Monarchy," so he called for more than one president. And he called for there to be no salary for the presidents, to avoid making "our Posts of Honour Places of Profit."

Benjamin Franklin lost on both points.

When the question arose of how each state, the small and the large ones, would be represented in the government, the debate became heated. Franklin suggested the delegates pause to pray, "That, henceforth prayers, imploring the assistance of Heaven and its blessing on our deliberations, be held in this Assembly every morning before we proceed to business."

Benjamin Franklin lost this point, too. "The Convention," he wrote in a note, "except three or four persons, thought prayers unnecessary."

On the question of representation, the small states wanted each state to have the same number of representatives. The larger states wanted the number to reflect the population of the state. Benjamin Franklin called for compromise. "When a broad table is to be made," he said, "and the edges of planks do not fit, the artist takes a little from both and makes a good joint. In like manner here both sides must part with some of their demands."

In the end, there was compromise. In the Senate each state was given the same number of representatives. In the House the number of representatives for each state would reflect its population.

"I agree to this Constitution, with all its faults—if they are such; because I think a general government necessary for us," Benjamin Franklin said when it was done. "I cannot help expressing a wish, that every member of the Convention who may still have objections to it, would with me on this occasion doubt a little of his own infallibility, and, to make *manifest* our *unanimity,* put his name to this Instrument."

Forty men signed the Constitution. By 1790 each of the thirteen original states ratified it. The proof of the genius of that document is that more than two hundred years later it continues to be the blueprint for our nation.

The last passion of Benjamin Franklin's life was for the abolition of slavery. Many years earlier, he had owned one or two slaves. They were servants in his house. But already in 1751, he spoke out against the institution. In 1787 he became president of "The Pennsylvania Society for Promoting the Abolition of Slavery, and the Relief of Free Negroes Unlawfully Held in Bondage." The nation's first abolition society, it was founded in 1774.

Benjamin Franklin called slavery "an atrocious debasement" and wrote a plan to improve the living conditions of free African Americans and to get them schooling and jobs.

Later in 1787, Benjamin Franklin fell down the stone steps just outside his house. He was badly bruised, and after that he stayed mostly in his bed. He began to put his financial house in order, to write his will.

Benjamin Franklin was a wealthy man. He had cash, bonds, and shares in the Bank of North America. Besides his house on Market Street, he owned seven other houses in Philadelphia and another in Boston. He owned land in Ohio, Georgia, and Nova Scotia. And he had a portrait of King Louis XVI of France surrounded with diamonds.

Benjamin Franklin left money and property to his children, grandchildren, and the Pennsylvania Hospital, and money to the people of Philadelphia and Boston.

"The king of France's picture," he wrote in his will, "set with four hundred and eight diamonds, I give to my daughter, Sarah Bache, requesting, however, that she not form any of those diamonds into ornaments either for herself or daughters, and thereby introduce or countenance the expensive, vain, and useless fashion of wearing jewels in this country."

"My fine crab-tree walking-stick," he wrote, "with a gold head, curiously wrought in the form of the cap of liberty, I give to my friend, and the friend of mankind, General Washington."

By 1790 Benjamin Franklin was in great pain. He had kidney troubles. He had trouble breathing. He was dying.

Then he rallied. The pain was mostly gone. His breathing improved. He got up, so that his bed could be made, so that he could "die in a decent manner." His daughter, Sally, said she hoped he was better now and would live many years more. Benjamin Franklin replied, "I hope not."

The pain returned and someone suggested he move a bit, to breathe easier. "A dying man," Benjamin Franklin replied, "can do nothing easy." Those were the last known words of Benjamin Franklin. He drifted into a deep sleep, a coma, and at eleven o'clock, on the night of April 17, 1790, surrounded by his family and close friends, he quietly died. Four days later he was buried on the grounds of Christ Church beside his wife and their son, Francis.

Franklin on his deathbed with one of his granddaughters, from a drawing by Victor A. Searles, c. 1897

Washington's sword and the walking stick Franklin left to Washington, from an engraving by Lossing and Barritt, c. 1850

"Fear not death," he had written in his 1740 almanac, "for the sooner we die, the longer we shall be immortal."

"Know it is our Duty," he wrote to his sister Jane Mecom in 1767, "to submit to the Divine Will."

Earlier, he wrote in his 1738 almanac,

> If you wou'd not be forgotten
> As soon as you are dead and rotten,
> Either write things worth reading,
> Or do things worth the writing.

Benjamin Franklin wrote many things worth reading. He did many things worth the writing. He was a great man, perhaps our greatest American.

On April 22 James Madison addressed Congress, then in session in New York City. He proposed this resolution: "The House being informed of the decease of Benjamin Franklin, a citizen whose native genius was not more an ornament to human nature than his various exertions of it have been precious to science, to freedom, and to his country, do resolve, as a mark of the veneration due to his memory, that the members wear the customary badge of mourning for one month."

The resolution passed unanimously.

Thomas Jefferson wrote of Franklin: "There appeared to me more respect and veneration attached to the character of Doctor Franklin in France than to that of any person in the same country, foreign or native.... When he left Passy (the village outside Paris where Franklin stayed) it seemed as if the village had lost its patriarch.... His death was an affliction which was to happen to us at some time or other. We have reason to be thankful he was so long spared."

On June 11, at the opening of the French National Legislature, Gabriel Riqueti Mirabeau, the great French speaker and politician, rose and announced, "Franklin is dead! The genius, that freed America and poured a flood of light over Europe, has returned to the bosom of the Divinity. The sage whom two worlds claim as their own, the man for whom the history of science and the history of empires contend with each other, held, without doubt, a high rank in the human race. . . . I propose that it be decreed, that the National Assembly, during three days, shall wear mourning for Benjamin Franklin."

Mirabeau's proposal was passed by acclamation.

According to the April 28, 1790, edition of the *Gazette of the United States,* at Franklin's funeral, "The concourse of spectators was greater than ever was known on a like occasion. It is computed that not less than 20,000 persons attended and witnessed the funeral. The order and silence which prevailed, during the Procession, deeply evinced the heartfelt sense, entertained by all classes of citizens, of the unparalleled virtues, talents, and services of the deceased."

With heavy hearts and tear-filled eyes, they said good-bye to Benjamin Franklin.

CHRONOLOGIES

BENJAMIN FRANKLIN, 1706–1790

1706	Born in Boston on January 17 (January 6, old-style calendar).
1714	Attends the Boston Latin School.
1716–1718	Works in father's soap and candle shop.
1718–1723	Works as apprentice in brother James's print shop.
1722	Writes his "Silence Dogood" letters for the *New-England Courant*.
1723	Runs away, first to New York, then to Philadelphia, where he takes a job in Samuel Keimer's print shop.
1724–1726	Works in London, first in Palmer's print shop, then in Watts's.
1726	Returns to Philadelphia after almost 80 days at sea.
1727	Founds, with friends, the Junto, a club "for mutual improvement."
1728	Opens his own print shop with a partner, Hugh Meredith.
1729	Buys the *Pennsylvania Gazette* from his former employer, Samuel Keimer.
1730	Marries Deborah Read.
1731	Son William born (year indefinite); sets up America's first subscription library.
1732	Son Francis Folger born; publishes in December the first of twenty-six *Poor Richard's Almanacks*, the 1733 edition.
1736	Son Francis Folger dies; organizes Philadelphia's Union Fire Company.
1736–1751	Serves as clerk of the Pennsylvania Assembly.
1737	Becomes Postmaster of Philadelphia.
1740	Makes first Franklin stove.
1743	Daughter Sarah (Sally) born.
1746	Begins experimenting with electricity.
1748	Retires from printing.
1751	Helps found the Academy of Philadelphia, which became University of Pennsylvania, and the Pennsylvania Hospital; initiates reform of Philadelphia police department.
1751–1764	Member of the Pennsylvania Assembly.
1752	Conducts kite experiment with his son, William, proving lightning is electricity.
1753–1774	Becomes Deputy Postmaster General of America.
1757–1762	Represents the Pennsylvania Assembly in London.
1764	Defends Native Americans in Philadelphia from the Paxton Boys.
1764–1775	Serves in London again, first as agent for Pennsylvania, then for Georgia, New Jersey, and Massachusetts.

1766   Witness in Parliament on Stamp Act issue.

1771–1789   Writes autobiography.

1774   Wife, Deborah Read, dies.

1775   Delegate to the Second Continental Congress.

1776   Serves on committee with Thomas Jefferson to draft the Declaration of Independence.

1776–1785   Serves in France.

1778   Helps negotiate an alliance with France, as well as a loan.

1782–1783   With John Adams and John Jay, negotiates peace treaty with England.

1787   Attends Constitutional Convention; becomes president of abolitionist group.

1790   Dies in Philadelphia on April 17.

THE NEW WORLD, 1706–1790

1714   Queen Anne of England dies. George I becomes king.

1727   King George I dies and is succeeded by George II.

1729   North and South Carolina established as separate royal colonies.

1732   Georgia becomes a colony, the last of the thirteen original colonies to be established.

1754–1763   The French and Indian War fought. The British forces eventually win.

1760   King George II of England dies and is succeeded by grandson, George III.

1765   Parliament passes Stamp Act.

1766   Parliament repeals Stamp Act.

1767   Parliament imposes taxes on American imports.

1770   Five American patriots killed in Boston Massacre.

1772   First Committees of Correspondence formed in Massachusetts.

1773   The Boston Tea Party.

1774   Parliament passes the Intolerable Acts.
         King Louis XV of France dies and is succeeded by grandson, Louis XVI.

1775–1783   American Revolution.

1776   Declaration of Independence signed.

1778   American colonies sign treaties with France and Holland. By an act of Congress, slaves may no longer be imported into the United States.

1781   Americans defeat the British at the Battle of Yorktown.

1783   The Treaty of Paris is signed, ending the Revolution.

1787   The United States Constitution is written.

1789   First United States Congress meets. George Washington elected president.

SOURCE NOTES

ABOUT THE NOTES AND IMAGES:

In these notes following the text, I include sources for information found in just one or two of the texts surveyed, but not for information found in almost every text. I also include information that I could not include in the text for reasons of continuity, but found too interesting to leave out.

Wherever possible, I give information on the artists and circa dates for the images reproduced to illustrate this book. Often, engravings from a later date were based on earlier paintings.

The quotes from Franklin, unless otherwise noted, are from his autobiography.

ABOUT THE SPELLINGS

I found Franklin's letter to his sister Jane Mecom on phonetic spelling and the explanation of eighteenth-century style in *Franklin's Vocabulary* by Lois Margaret MacLaurin.

1. MORE A KING

It was Sir James MacIntosh in 1812 who described Franklin as a singular man of peculiar character and extraordinary talents and Lord Brougham in 1839 who described Franklin as having a mind that "soared above the clouds." Both statements appear in the appendix of James Parton's 1864 two-volume *Life and Times of Benjamin Franklin*.

Franklin arrived in Paris to represent the United States in December 1776, shortly before his seventy-first birthday.

Franklin described himself as "an old man with grey hair" in a letter to a friend, Polly Stevenson Hewson, the daughter of his English landlady. That letter was written in the midst of the American Revolution. Franklin also wrote, "I must contrive to get you to America. I want all my Friends out of that wicked Country."

Although the people of Paris saw Franklin's bare head as a statement of independence from rules of dress, it may simply have been a matter of good sense. Wearing a wig irritated a skin condition he had at the time.

M. L. Weems

The earliest reference I found for the wig story was in the 1829 biography *The Life of Benjamin Franklin with Many Choice Anecdotes and Admirable Sayings of this Great Man* by M. L. Weems. It also appears in the more reliable Parton biography.

Horace Greeley (1811–1872) made his speech in 1862, at the unveiling in Boston of a statue honoring Benjamin Franklin. "His newspaper," Greeley said of Franklin, "his almanac, his electrical researches, his parliamentary service, his diplomacy, were the best of their time." Greeley also said that Franklin was "the consummate type and flowering of human nature under the skies of colonial America." My source for Greeley's speech is the appendix to Parton's biography.

2. THE FRANKLINS

King's Handbook of Boston, published in 1883, tells what happened to the "humble little house which stood on Milk Street," Franklin's birthplace. "The old house stood a hundred and twenty years, respected as one of the most notable landmarks; and its destruction by fire, in 1811, was keenly regretted, especially by the older citizens."

Benjamin Franklin's birth date, January 17, is from the "New Style" Gregorian calendar, adopted in the American colonies in 1752 and still in use. His birth date in the "Old Style" calendar was January 6.

The snow was so deep in Boston the day Benjamin Franklin was born that one man was lost in it and died.

Benjamin Franklin was named for his father's brother, a devout man. The elder Benjamin often went to church with paper and pen and wrote down every word of the minister's sermons. He accumulated many volumes of these handwritten speeches and read them over and over again. Uncle Benjamin suffered real tragedy. By 1706 Uncle Benjamin's wife had died and so had nine of his ten children. For a while, beginning in 1715, when he first came to the American colonies, Uncle Benjamin lived in Boston with the Franklins and took a special interest in his namesake.

In 1662, during the reign of Charles II (1660–1685) of England, it was mandated that every clergyman endorse the king as supreme in all things religious and embrace the entire *Book of Common Prayer.* The 1664 Conventicle Act made any religious gathering in a private home illegal, punishable by a fine, imprisonment, or expulsion. In 1665 the Five-Mile Act prohibited any nonconformist minister to come within five miles of any English town. The rewards were great for anyone who turned in his neighbor. It took only the testimony of a single witness to convict a private worshiper, and that witness was rewarded with one-third of whatever fine was set. Quakers suffered the most during this time of persecution.

It was not unusual for women in eighteenth-century America to give birth to (and sometimes bury) many children. With his two wives, Josiah Franklin fathered seventeen children. Governor William Phipps (1651–1695) of Massachusetts was one of twenty-six children, all of the same mother. The Reverend Cotton Mather (1663–1728) married twice and had fifteen children.

It was Benjamin's half-brother Josiah who went off to sea. I found that he returned in a 1760 letter Benjamin Franklin wrote to his sister Jane Mecom. "I remember these thirteen (some of us very young) all at one table, when an Entertainment was made in our House on the Occasion of the Return of Brother Josiah, who had been absent in East Indies, and unheard of for nine years." The letter appears in the Library of America collection *Franklin Writings*.

3. APPRENTICE PRINTER

The first American newspaper, *Publick Occurrences Both Forreign and Domestick*, appeared in 1690 in Boston. After one issue, colonial authorities declared it illegal: the publisher did not have a government license to report the news. In December 1719, one day after the *Boston Gazette* was published, to become the second regularly published newspaper in the colonies, the *American Weekly Mercury* appeared in Philadelphia and became the third.

During his few years as a vegetarian, Franklin considered eating fish "as a kind of unprovoked murder." But on his first trip out of Boston, the people he was with caught some cod and "when this came hot out of the frying pan, it smelt admirably well." When the fish were cut open, Franklin "saw smaller fish taken out of their stomachs; then thought I, 'If you eat one another, I don't see why we mayn't eat you.' So I dined upon cod very heartily . . . returning only now and then occasionally to a vegetable diet."

The Reverend Mather's arguments with James Franklin and the *New-England Courant* appeared in the rival newspaper, the *Boston News-Letter*.

Advertisements for runaway apprentices and slaves were common in colonial newspapers, so Franklin surely thought often about running away. His destination, if he intended to remain a printer, could only be New York or Philadelphia, at the time the only other towns in the colonies with print shops.

4. RUNAWAY

James Franklin's *New-England Courant* folded after a few years and James moved on to Newport, Rhode Island, where he started that colony's first newspaper. It was while James was in Rhode Island that he and Benjamin reconciled. At the time,

James was in poor health. When he died, he wanted Benjamin to take care of his ten-year-old son and teach him how to be a printer. Benjamin promised his brother he would, and he did. "Thus it was," Benjamin later wrote, "that I made my brother ample amends."

My description of Deborah Read is based on two sources. In his 1926 biography of Franklin, *Benjamin Franklin: The First Civilized American*, Phillips Russell described her as "broadly built, and full bosomed, with a kind of vigorous beauty." Russell also wrote, "Witnesses have left testimony as to her sharp tongue." In his 1938 biography, *Benjamin Franklin*, Carl Van Doren described her as a "sturdy, handsome, high-coloured woman, untaught and sometimes turbulent." The physical description of Benjamin Franklin comes from Sydney George Fisher's 1898 book, *The True Benjamin Franklin.*

The information on eighteenth-century London comes from John Brewer's book, *The Pleasures of the Imagination*. The dangerous nature of London life is described in Bernard Fay's 1929 biography, *Franklin: The Apostle of Modern Times.* "Robberies, murders and immoralities of every kind filled the columns of the newspapers," Fay wrote. "The newspapers recounted these outrages with exaggerated details, and for months the conventional fourth page was filled with advertisements promising high rewards to those who could deliver up the guilty ones."

Surely one reason for Franklin's great strength and his ability to carry heavy type was that at about five feet ten inches, he was tall for his time. He also had rounded shoulders and muscular arms.

Franklin's 1726 resolutions while sailing to Philadelphia are from Thomas Fleming's *Benjamin Franklin: A Biography in His Own Words.*

5. THE BUSY BODY

I found the Busy Body letters in the Library of America's book of Franklin's writings. In another letter Franklin wrote a rather complicated message in praise of virtue: "If we were as industrious to become Good, as to make ourselves Great, we should become really Great by being Good. . . . It is a Grand Mistake to think of being Great without Goodness; and I pronounce it as certain, *that there was never yet a truly Great Man that was not at the same Time truly Virtuous.*"

"Perfuming the beards" ceremony is described in the fourth Busy Body regarding the "*Turkish* manner of entertaining Visitors." At the end of a visit comes the "Perfuming the beards of the Company; a Ceremony which is perform'd in this manner.

They have for the purpose a small Silver Chaffing-Dish, cover'd with a Lid full of Holes, and fixed upon a handsome Plate. In this they put some fresh Coals, and upon them a piece of *Lignum Aloes*, and shutting it up, the Smoak immediately ascends with a grateful Odour thro' the Holes of the Cover. The Smoak is held under every one's Chin, and offer'd as it were a Sacrifice to his Beard."

Of the first issues of Franklin's newspaper, James Parton wrote more than a century later, "Indeed, no newspaper of the United States, in the year 1861, is printed so legibly or so elegantly as the *Pennsylvania Gazette* of 1729." Parton declared that the *Gazette* was "the best newspaper published in the colonies."

Having an illegitimate child was not officially tolerated in colonial Philadelphia. The required punishment was twenty-one lashes at the public whipping post. There is no evidence that it was meted out to Benjamin Franklin.

Among the visitors to Philadelphia in 1736 who fled during the smallpox epidemic were representatives from six Native American nations who came to sign a treaty.

I found the excerpt from Franklin's letter to his mother in Paul Leicester Ford's *The Many-Sided Franklin* and Franklin's note on the marriage of Sally in Van Doren's biography.

My source for Peggy Ross's deathbed request that Richard Bache, her intended husband, marry Sally Franklin is *The Private Franklin: The Man and His Family* by Claude-Anne Lopez and Eugenia W. Herbert. They added that in 1866, Elizabeth Duane Gillespie, Sally and Richard Bache's granddaughter, wanted to mark the one hundredth anniversary of Peggy Ross's plea and subsequent death with a family picnic. The idea was dropped by more thoughtful family members.

At the end of his two-volume biography, Parton quoted Mr. William Duane of Philadelphia, Franklin's great-grandson, with information on Franklin's descendants. Duane reported that Franklin's great-grandson Hartman Bache married Maria Meade, the sister of General George Meade, who led the victorious Union Army at the Battle of Gettysburg. Franklin's great-granddaughter Frances Sergeant married the son of Commodore Perry.

6. FIRST CITIZEN OF PHILADELPHIA

Around Philadelphia the Junto was known as "The Leather Apron Club" because many of its members were tradesmen, workers who wore leather aprons. My source for the questions posed at the Junto Club is Parton's biography. The questions listed here were apparently Franklin's. They were quoted by Parton from a journal then in the possession of one of Franklin's grandchildren. The letter Franklin wrote from France can be found in Ford's biography.

"We derive from tradition a pretty story," Parton wrote in his biography, "respecting the introduction of Plaster of Paris as a fertilizer." Franklin demonstrated to farmers its effectiveness by writing with plaster in large letters, "THIS HAS BEEN PLASTERED" in a field along the side of a road. The white powder soon disappeared and the words *This has been plastered,* were spelled out in emerald green grass. Van Doren wrote this demonstration was "possibly" done in 1786, when Franklin was eighty years old.

7. POOR RICHARD

According to Phillips Russell's biography, there were seven other almanacs being published in Philadelphia in 1733, when *Poor Richard's Almanack* first appeared.

The title for Franklin's almanac may have come, in part, from the comic *Poor Robin's Almanac.* The name Richard Saunders may have come from a real person, the author of *The English Apollo,* a serious almanac published in England.

Colonial Americans truly relied on their almanacs. "The authors didn't dare take too many liberties," Bernard Fay wrote in his 1929 biography. If they did, their readers might turn against them, as one did against Sower of Philadelphia. One day an angry farmer came into Sower's shop and demanded he be paid for damages to his clothes and goods. Early that morning, after checking the Sower almanac, he found there would be "good weather" that day. He set off for the city with his produce and some woolen goods his wife had knitted. By noon the rain started and continued the rest of the day. That night, he arrived in Philadelphia soaked. His clothes and goods were ruined. He went straight to Sower and protested. "O Friend, Friend, be not thus angry," Sower told the farmer, "although It was I that made the almanac, the Lord God made the weather."

Franklin wrote in his autobiography that his original list of virtues included only twelve, "but a Quaker friend having kindly informed me that I was generally thought proud; that my pride showed itself frequently in conversation; that I was not content with being in the right when discussing any point, but was overbearing, and rather insolent of which he convinced me by mentioning several instances; I determined endeavoring to cure myself; if I could, of this vice or folly among the rest, and I added Humility to my list."

The account of Franklin's 1767 experience at the French Academy, when he unknowingly applauded himself, appears in Ford's biography.

8. EXPERIMENTS WITH ELECTRICITY

At about the same time, 1745 to 1746, Pieter van Musschenbroek (1692–1761) made his Leyden jar, Ewald Georg von Kleist (1700–1748), a German inventor, made a similar device called the Kleistian jar. Both were glass jars with water inside, about half of the jar wrapped inside and out with metal foil, a cork stopper at the opening, and a wire or nail going through the stopper with one end in the water. Something was then used to produce static electricity. It was touched to the exposed end of the wire or nail and the electric current traveled through the wire or nail and was stored in the water.

Franklin taught some of his friends what he knew about electricity. One friend, Ebenezer Kinnersley (1711–1778), rigged an image of King George II (1683–1760, reign 1727–1760) ("God preserve him," Franklin added when he wrote the story, for he was still loyal to the king) so that anyone who tried to take the crown off the king's head felt a powerful electrical shock.

In writing the reactions of some ministers to Franklin's invention of the lightning rod, James Parton recounted an entry in John Adams's diary of a doctor who would "nail and foam" against lightning rods as an attempt to "control the artillery of Heaven." Parton also recounted an advertisement for a lecture on electricity given by Franklin's friend Kinnersley in which he intended to show that erecting a lightning rod was not "inconsistent with any of the principles either of natural or revealed religion." Perhaps Kinnersley's lecture had some standing with the religious community, since he was a Baptist minister.

It was Peter Collinson (1694–1768), the naturalist and lover of antiquities, someone Franklin met on his 1726 visit to London, who wrote the "feather in the cap" letter. Collinson later became the London agent for Franklin's Library Company of Philadelphia. In 1746 he sent Franklin an electrical tube with directions on how to use it. Franklin's response to Collinson's remarks were in a 1753 letter to Jared Eliot, another friend, which I found in the Fleming book.

9. GENERAL FRANKLIN

The first shots of the French and Indian War were fired on May 28, 1754, by soldiers under the command of twenty-two-year-old Lieutenant Colonel George Washington. It was the first battle for young Washington. According to his report, in the battle twelve Frenchmen and one of Washington's soldiers were killed. "I fortunately escaped without any wound," he wrote in a May 31 letter to his brother. He also wrote, "I heard the bullets whistle, and, believe me, there is something charming in the sound."

The cry "Taxation without representation is tyranny!" is attributed to James Otis (1725–1783) of Massachusetts, although, according to some historians, his actual words were, "No parts of His Majesty's dominions can be taxed without their consent."

"This General was I think a brave Man," Franklin later wrote of General Edward Braddock, "and might probably have made a Figure as a good Officer in some European War. But he had too much self-confidence, too high an Opinion of the Validity of Regular Troops, and too much a mean One of both Americans and Indians."

Pennsylvania means Penn's Woods. It was named for Admiral Sir William Penn (1621–1670), the father of William Penn (1644–1718), founder of the colony. In 1681 King Charles II gave twenty-six million acres of Pennsylvania land to William Penn. Penn's descendants lived in England.

10. FROM THE OLD WORLD TO THE NEW

William Strahan (1715–1785), a friend from Franklin's printing days in London, was the one who urged Deborah Franklin to join her husband in London. According to the Lopez and Herbert biography, Franklin later wrote to Deborah that his friend offered to bet he could get Deborah to come to London, but Franklin refused the bet. "I will not pick his pocket," he wrote to Deborah. He was sure that because of her fear of sea voyages she would not come. Some historians also suggest that Deborah might have remained in Philadelphia because she feared she would not measure up to the elegant women of London.

The remarkable fact that Deborah Read Franklin seldom left the Market Street area and only went as far away as Lancaster, Pennsylvania, and Woodbridge, New Jersey, appears in the Lopez and Herbert biography.

In 1757 Franklin said good-bye to Deborah, Sally, and the other members of their household—Deborah's aged mother, one or two nieces, and an old nurse named "Goody" Smith. He left, according to the Van Doren biography, just as work was beginning on their new three-story brick house on Market Street.

According to scholars, Stonehenge was built and rebuilt in three stages beginning about five thousand years ago and was probably used as a tribal gathering place and religious center. It remains one of England's most popular tourist sites.

According to *American National Biography,* William Franklin "proved an able governor" of New Jersey. During his fourteen-year term, he pardoned women jailed for adultery, ended the practice of jailing people who were unable to pay their debts, had bridges built in New Jersey and its roads improved, and established in Burlington County the first reservation for Native Americans.

The Franklin "I am going home" letter was written to his friend Lord Kames. I found it in *Benjamin Franklin* by John T. Morse, Jr. Lord Kames (1696–1792) was a lawyer, judge, and philosopher.

11. THE PAXTON BOYS

The "My wife and daughter" letter was to Lord Kames. Excerpts of it appear in the Parton biography.

Franklin reported in his pamphlet that before the massacre of the Conestogas, the leader of the tribe was warned that some English might come to harm his people. He would not believe it. "There are Indians," he said, "who would kill me and mine, if they could get at us, for my friendship to the English; but the English will wrap me in their matchcoat, and secure me from all danger." Franklin wrote, "How unfortunately he was mistaken!"

In 1763 the governor general of British North America suggested that blankets be tainted with smallpox germs and distributed among the tribes. While there is no record that this was done, as reported in the Van Doren biography of Franklin, it is an indication of the terrible state of relations at the time between white men and Native Americans.

In the mid-1700s eight of the thirteen colonies—Massachusetts, Connecticut, Rhode Island, New Hampshire, New York, New Jersey, Delaware, and Virginia—had royal charters. The remaining five—Pennsylvania, Maryland, North Carolina, South Carolina, and Georgia—had proprietary characters: they were governed by people other than the king.

12. THE MOTHER OF MISCHIEFS

Franklin's "I took every step in my power" Stamp Act letter was sent to Charles Thomson of Philadelphia and written on July 11, 1765, almost four months after the act was passed in Parliament. Thomson (1729–1824) was later secretary of the Continental Congress.

With the passage of the Stamp Act, Franklin must have sensed that there was real trouble ahead. According to James Parton and John Morse in their biographies, Franklin told an American friend who was on his way back to the colonies, "Go home and tell your countrymen to get children as fast as they can." He knew that one day's children would be the next day's soldiers.

I found excerpts of the 1765 letters from John Hughes and Deborah Franklin in Fleming's biography. Franklin's 1766 letter to his wife appears in the Library of America's collection of Franklin's writing.

It was the American writer and poet Ralph Waldo Emerson (1803–1882) who wrote in 1836, at the dedication of a monument to the first battle of the Revolution,

> By the rude bridge that arched the flood,
> Their flag to April's breeze unfurled,
> Here once the embattled farmers stood,
> And fired the shot heard round the world.

Thomas Hutchinson (1711–1780), the royal governor of Massachusetts and author of the infamous letters calling for a stronger British hand, was American-born, a descendant of Anne Hutchinson (1591–1643), the rebellious Puritan leader. After the Boston Tea Party, he moved to England and became an advisor to King George III.

I found copies of Franklin's December 25, 1773, letter admitting he had sent the Hutchinson letters to Boston in the Parton and Morse biographies.

My source for the Samuel Johnson (1709–1784) quote calling Franklin "the master of mischief" is Phillips Russell's biography. According to Russell, Johnson also said he was "willing to love all mankind except an American."

13. THE BROKEN VASE

The story Franklin told Jefferson of the John Thompson sign appears in many places, including the Parton biography.

A legend tells that before he signed the Declaration of Independence, John Hancock said, "We must be unanimous. There must be no pulling different ways. We must all hang together," and that Benjamin Franklin replied, "Yes, we must, indeed, all hang together, or, most assuredly, we shall all hang separately." According to historian Dumas Malone in *The Story of the Declaration of Independence*, this exchange between Hancock and Franklin first appeared in print about fifty years after

Franklin's death, "much too late for him to deny it." Parton qualified his retelling of Hancock's call to the Congress to be unanimous and Franklin's reply with "Hancock is reported to have said," and "Tradition assigns to Franklin the well-known, witty reply."

The dialogue between Franklin and Howe is from the notes of Henry Strachey, Howe's secretary, as quoted in the Parton biography.

Along with saying, at age seventy, "I am old and good for nothing," as recounted in the Ford biography, Franklin once wrote, "For my own part, I do not find that I grow any older. Being arrived at seventy, and considering that by traveling farther in the same road I should probably be led to the grave, I stopped short, turned about, and walked back again; which done these four years, you may now call me sixty-six."

14. HUZZAH! HUZZAH!

Edward Gibbon

By 1776 the English historian Edward Gibbon (1737–1794) had completed the first volume of his five-volume study, *The History of the Decline and Fall of the Roman Empire.* Gibbon retold what he called "an anecdote of some point, and not too improbable for belief." According to the story, in December 1776, on his journey from the coast of France to Paris, Franklin and Gibbon spent the night in the same inn. In a note passed to Gibbon, Franklin asked to meet with the historian, but the Englishman refused. He would not meet with anyone in revolt against his king. Franklin wrote a second note, this time telling Gibbon that when he was ready to write about the *decline and fall of the British Empire,* "as he expects it soon," he would be happy to help in the research.

In February 1778, when Franklin signed the Treaty of Alliance, in a bit of irony he surely enjoyed, he wore the same suit he had worn when he sat before a committee of the British Parliament in 1774 and was insulted by Alexander Wedderburn (1733–1805), the solicitor general. According to his friend William Wilberforce, as quoted in the Parton biography, Franklin wore the suit again in 1783, when he signed the Treaty of Paris.

Franklin's letter about the ladies of Paris appears in the Van Doren biography. I found that Franklin played chess with Madame Brillon while she was in her bath in the Samual Eliot Morison biography of John Paul Jones. The fact that the bathtub was covered and the details about Madame Helvétius's many pets are in the Fay biography. My source for the letters Franklin wrote to his daughter, Sally, William Strahan, and the Reverend Samuel Mather is the Library of America's collection of his writings.

Mrs. Adams's description of Madame Helvétius was in a letter she wrote. Excerpts from the letter appear in John Bach McMaster's 1890 *Benjamin Franklin as a Man of Letters*.

While Franklin was negotiating the treaty, a new craze was beginning in France: ballooning. In June 1783 a cloth-and-paper smoke-filled balloon went up east of Paris. Then, very early on the morning of August 27, just one week before Franklin signed the Treaty of Paris, he was one of some fifty thousand people in the Champ de Mars, a field near the Seine, to witness the first balloon rise over Paris. "It diminish'd in Apparent Magnitude as it rose," Franklin wrote in a letter, "till it enter'd the Clouds, when it seem'd to me scarce bigger than an Orange, and soon after became invisible, the Clouds concealing it." At the time, someone asked Franklin, "What is the use of this new invention?" Franklin replied, "What is the use of a new-born child?"

From 1777 to 1782, according to Parton, Franklin collected for America a total of twenty-six million francs from France, money which saved the Revolution.

Franklin's portrait has been on U.S. postage stamps and currency, including one of the first stamps issued in 1847, large-sized $50 notes from 1874 to 1880, the half dollar coin from 1948 to 1963, and this $100 bill.

15. A DYING MAN

I found this description of Franklin's house in Parton's biography. He quoted Dr. Manasseh Cutler, who visited Franklin in 1787. The house "stands up a court, at some distance from the street... He invited me into his library, which is likewise his study. It is a very large chamber and high-studded. The walls are covered with bookshelves, filled with books...I presume this is the largest and by far the best private library in America." During that visit, Franklin also showed him "a curiosity he had just received, and with which he was much pleased. It was a snake with two heads, preserved in a phial."

A speech against Jews was attributed to Franklin and was said to have been written during the time of the Constitutional Convention. According to Van Doren, the speech was forged and first appeared in 1934, almost one hundred and fifty years after Franklin's death.

My source for the resolution of Congress, Mirabeau's speech, and the *Gazette's* description of the funeral is Parton's biography.

Franklin often said he would like to revisit the earth a hundred years after his death, to see what improvements and discoveries had been made in his absence.

RECOMMENDED WEB SITES

http://www.earlyamerica.com
Click on "Enter the World of Early America," then "The Lives of Early Americans" to find Benjamin Franklin's autobiography. To see other colonial documents, click on "Pages from the Past."

http://www.fi.edu
The Franklin Institute Science Museum Online. Here, click on "Learning Resources," then "Benjamin Franklin, Glimpses of the Man."

http://www.tlc.ai.org
The Access Indiana Teaching and Learning Center. On the topic list, click on "F," then on "Franklin, Benjamin" for lots of information and illustrations, including reproductions from *Poor Richard's Almanack*.

http://www.mos.org/sln/toe
The Museum of Science's Theater of Electricity. Check its online exhibits for information on Franklin's kite experiment.

SELECTED BIBLIOGRAPHY

Abbott, John C. *The French Revolution of 1789.* New York: Harper, 1887.

Adams, Abigail. *Letters of Mrs. Adams,* volume 1. Boston: Charles C. Little and James Brown, 1840.

Aldridge, Alfred Owen. *Benjamin Franklin: Philosopher and Man.* Philadelphia: Lippincott, 1965.

Amacher, Richard E. *Benjamin Franklin.* New Haven: College and University Press, 1962.

American Revolution in New York, The. Albany: University of the State of New York, 1926.

American Weekly Mercury, Philadelphia: 1719–1724.

Belcher, Henry. *The First American Civil War.* London: Macmillan, 1911.

Boston News-Letter, 1704–1719.

Bowen, Catherine Drinker. *The Most Dangerous Man in America: Scenes from the Life of Benjamin Franklin.* Boston: Atlantic Monthly Press Books, 1974.

Brands, H. W. *The First American: The Life and Times of Benjamin Franklin.*
    New York: Doubleday, 2000.

Brewer, John. *The Pleasures of the Imagination: English Culture of the
    Eighteenth Century.* New York: Farrar, Straus and Giroux, 1997.

Bridenbaugh, Carl. *Cities in the Wilderness.* New York: Knopf, 1955.

Brooks, Eldridge S. *The True Story of Benjamin Franklin.* Boston: Lothrop,
    Lee and Shepard, 1898.

Chancellor, E. Beresford. *The Eighteenth Century in London.* London:
    B. T. Batsford, 1920.

Clark, Ronald W. *Benjamin Franklin: A Biography.* New York:
    Random House, 1983.

Cooke, Jacob Ernest, ed. *North American Colonies.* New York: Scribner, 1993.

Dupuy, Trevor N., and Gay M. Hammerman, eds. *People and Events of the
    American Revolution.* New York: R. R. Bowker, 1974.

Earle, Alice Morse. *Child Life in Colonial Days.* New York: Macmillan, 1899;
    Stockbridge, Massachusetts: Berkshire House, 1993.

Fay, Bernard. *Franklin: The Apostle of Modern Times.* Boston: Little, Brown, 1929.

Federal Writers' Project. *Massachusetts: A Guide to its Places and People.*
    Boston: Houghton Mifflin, 1937.

Fisher, Sydney George. *The True Benjamin Franklin.* Philadelphia:
    Lippincott, 1898.

——— *The True William Penn.* Philadelphia: Lippincott, 1907.

Fitzpatrick, John C., ed. *The Writings of George Washington.* Washington,
    D.C.: U.S. Government Printing Office, 1939.

Fleming, Thomas. *Benjamin Franklin: A Biography in His Own Words.*
    New York: Newsweek, 1972.

Ford, Paul Leicester. *The Many-Sided Franklin.* New York: Century, 1899.

Franklin, Benjamin. *The Complete Poor Richard's Almanacks,* volumes 1 and 2.
    Barre, Massachusetts: Imprint Society, 1970.

——— *Writing: Essays, Articles, Bagatelles, and Letters,
    Poor Richard's Almanack, Autobiography.* New York:
    Library of America, 1987.

Garraty, John A., and Mark C. Carnes, eds. *American National Biography,*
    24 volumes. New York and Oxford: Oxford University Press, 1999.

Hart, Albert Buchnell. *New American History.* New York: American Book, 1921.

Hawke, David Freeman. *Everyday Life in Early America.* New York:
    Harper and Row, 1988.

Holliday, Carl. *Woman's Life: in Colonial Days.* New York: Frederick Ungar, 1960.

Jefferson, Thomas. *Jefferson Writings*. New York: Library of America, 1984.

Knight, Sarah Kemble. *The Journal of Madam Knight*. Boston: David R. Godine, 1972.

Kobre, Sidney. *The Development of the Colonial Newspaper*. Gloucester, Massachusetts: Peter Smith, 1960.

Lemay, J. A. Leo, ed. *Benjamin Franklin: Writings*. New York: Library of America, 1987.

Lengyel, Cornel. *Four Days in July*. New York: Doubleday, 1958.

Lincoln, Charles Henry. *Correspondence of William Shirley*. New York: Macmillan, 1912.

Lopez, Claude-Anne, and Eugenia W. Herbert. *The Private Franklin: The Man and His Family*. New York: W. W. Norton, 1975.

Lossing, Benson J. *The Pictorial Field-Book of the Revolution*, 2 volumes. New York: Harper, 1852 and 1860.

MacLaurin, Lois Margaret. *Franklin's Vocabulary*. Garden City, New York: Doubleday, 1928.

McMaster, John Bach. *Benjamin Franklin as a Man of Letters*. Cambridge, Massachusetts: Riverside Press, 1890.

Madison, James. *Madison: Writings*. New York: Library of America, Penguin Putnam, 1999.

Malone, Dumas. *The Story of the Declaration of Independence*. New York: Oxford University Press, 1954.

Morison, Samuel Eliot. *John Paul Jones: A Sailor's Biography*. Boston: Atlantic Monthly Press, 1959.

Morse, John T. *Benjamin Franklin*. Boston: Houghton Mifflin, 1889.

Oswald, John Clyde. *Benjamin Franklin, Printer*. New York: Associated Advertising Clubs of the World/Doubleday, 1917.

Parton, James. *Life and Times of Benjamin Franklin*, 2 volumes. New York: Mason Brothers, 1864.

Pennypacker, Samuel Whitaker. *Pennsylvania: The Keystone*. Philadelphia: Sower, 1914.

Purvis, Thomas L. *Colonial America to 1763*. New York: Facts on File, 1999.

Randall, Willard. *A Little Revenge: Benjamin Franklin and His Son*. Boston: Little, Brown, 1984.

Russell, Phillips. *Benjamin Franklin: The First Civilized American*. New York: Brentano's, 1926.

Schoenbrun, David. *Triumph in Paris*. New York: Harper & Row, 1976.

Schroeder, John Frederick, and Benson John Lossing. *Life and Times of Washington.* Albany, New York: Washington Press, 1903. First printed in 1857–1861.

Stowell, Marion Barber. *Early American Almanacs: The Colonial Weekday Bible.* New York: Burt Franklin, 1977.

Van Doren, Carl. *Benjamin Franklin.* New York: Viking Press, 1938.

Weems, M. L. *The Life of Benjamin Franklin.* Philadelphia: Uriah Hunt and Son, 1829.

Wright, Esmond. *Franklin of Philadelphia.* Cambridge: Harvard University Press, 1986.

ILLUSTRATION CREDITS

Abbott, John C. *The French Revolution of 1789*: p. 2

Adams, Abigail. *Letters of Mrs. Adams,* volume 1: p. 84 (bottom)

Belcher, Henry. *The First American Civil War*: p. 5

Brooks, Eldridge S. *The True Story of Benjamin Franklin*: pp. 4 (both), 9, 13, 18, 21, 23, 32 (top), 98, 101 (top)

Chancellor, E. Beresford. *The Eighteenth Century in London*: p. 25

Fisher, Sydney George. *The True Benjamin Franklin*: endpapers, pp. 3, 31, 32 (bottom), 33 (top) 62
    —— *The True William Penn*: p. 64 (both)

Hart, Albert Buchnell. *New American History*: pp. 19, 54 (top), 73, 88

Library of Congress: pp. 11, 12, 20, 37, 49, 53, 55, 65, 86, 96

Lincoln, Charles Henry. *Correspondence of William Shirley*: p. 57

Lossing, Benson J. *The Pictorial-Field Book of the Revolution*: pp. 26 (top), 72, 76, 77, 87 (both), 90, 91, 93, 94, 98, 99, 101 (bottom), 106, 116

Parton, James. *Life and Times of Benjamin Franklin,* 2 volumes: pp. 1, 26 (bottom), 33 (bottom), 34, 54 (bottom), 82, 89

Pennypacker, Samuel Whitaker. *Pennsylvania, The Keystone:* p. 68

Oswald, John Clyde. *Benjamin Franklin Printer:* pp. 17, 40, 43, 45, 50, 57 (top), 69

Schroeder, John Frederick and Benson J. Lossing. *Life and Times of Washington:* frontispiece, pp. 59, 75, 81, 84 (top), 85

Yale University Art Gallery, Trumbull Collection: jacket

INDEX

(Page numbers in italics refer to illustrations)